Julius Payer

New Lands within the Arctic Circle

Narrative of the Discoveries of the Austrian ship

Julius Payer

New Lands within the Arctic Circle

Narrative of the Discoveries of the Austrian ship

ISBN/EAN: 9783337330408

Printed in Europe, USA, Canada, Australia, Japan

Cover: Foto ©ninafisch / pixelio.de

More available books at **www.hansebooks.com**

NEW LANDS
WITHIN THE ARCTIC CIRCLE.

*NARRATIVE OF THE DISCOVERIES
OF THE AUSTRIAN SHIP "TEGETTHOFF"
IN THE YEARS 1872-1874.*

BY

JULIUS PAYER,

ONE OF THE COMMANDERS OF THE EXPEDITION.

WITH MAPS AND NUMEROUS ILLUSTRATIONS FROM DRAWINGS
BY THE AUTHOR.

Translated from the German, with the Author's Approbation.

IN TWO VOLUMES.

VOL. I.

London:
MACMILLAN AND CO.
1876.

LONDON:
R. CLAY, SONS, AND TAYLOR, PRINTERS,
BREAD STREET HILL,
QUEEN VICTORIA STREET.

AUTHOR'S PREFACE.

In laying this book before the Public I desire, in the first instance, to acknowledge without reserve my sense of the great merits of my colleague, Lieutenant Weyprecht. The reader of the following pages will learn with what unwearied, though fruitless energy, he struggled to free the *Tegetthoff* from her icy prison, and what dauntless courage and unfailing command of resources he displayed in our hazardous retreat from the abandoned ship, till the moment of our happy rescue. The order and discipline maintained on board ship, and in the terrible march over the Frozen Ocean, as well as in the perilous boat voyage after leaving the ice-barrier, were mainly due to his distinguished abilities. He had supreme command of the expedition, as long as its duties were strictly nautical; when the operations of sledging and surveying began, I had the responsibility of a separate and independent command.

Nor ought I to be slow to pay my tribute of respect to the perseverance and constant self-denial of Lieutenant Brosch and Midshipman Orel. It would be difficult to determine, whether they shone more as officers of the ship, or as observers of scientific phenomena. The highly important duty of managing the stores and provisions was discharged also by Lieutenant Brosch with a conscientiousness that secured the confidence of all.

To the watchful skill of Dr. Kepes we owed it, that the health and constitution of the members of the expedition suffered so little from all their hardships and privations.

The conduct of the crew was on the whole praiseworthy. Their obedience to command, their perseverance and resolution shown on every occasion, will be cited as an example of what these virtues and qualities can achieve amid the most appalling dangers and trials.

With regard to my narrative, I make no claim for it founded on its literary excellence; rather I sue for indulgence to its manifold shortcomings. I have not written for the man of science, though I have not shunned a few scientific details. Nor have I aimed at presenting a record, which might be profitable to those who shall follow us in the same career of discovery, though some hints will be found in my pages which will not be without their use to those, who may consult them for information and guidance. Rather I have endeavoured to narrate our sufferings, adventures, and discoveries in a manner which shall be interesting to the general reader who reads to amuse himself.

The magnetical and meteorological observations, so carefully taken and tabulated by Weyprecht, Brosch, and Orel, together with the sketches of the Fauna of the Frozen Ocean, drawn by myself from the collection of Dr. Kepes, were presented to the Imperial Academy of Sciences at Vienna, and will in due time be published under the auspices of that august body.

PRELIMINARY NOTICE BY THE TRANSLATOR.

It will be interesting to English readers to learn a few particulars concerning the two leaders of the Austrian North Polar Expeditions. Carl Weyprecht was born in Hesse-Darmstadt in 1838, and in his eighteenth year entered the Austrian navy. Ten years afterwards he was present at the action between the Austrian and Italian fleets at Lissa—July 20, 1866; was promoted to the rank of lieutenant of the second class, and *decorated* with the order of the Iron Cross in recognition of his services in that battle. It was shortly after this, that Weyprecht volunteered to take the command of a small vessel, manned by only four seamen, which was to sail from Hammerfest to explore the Arctic Ocean. This dauntless offer was the basis of the first German North Polar expedition. When, however, permission to act in this capacity was obtained, Lieutenant Weyprecht was erving on board the Austrian frigate *Elizabeth*.

which formed one of the squadron sent by the Austrian Government to bring home the body of the ill-fated Maximilian. Immediately on his return to Europe he repaired to Gotha, eager to place his services at the command of the expedition which had meantime been planned by Petermann and a committee of patrons of Arctic exploration. But unhappily, just at this moment his health, which had suffered from fever caught at New Orleans, failed, and the command of the expedition, known as the first German North Polar expedition (May 24— October 10, 1868), was undertaken by Captain Koldewey. It was only in 1871, that he recovered his health, and in the June of that year began, in the *Isbjörn*, his life of Arctic experience and discovery. In the following year, 1872, he was appointed to the naval command of the expedition which sailed in the *Tegetthoff*, whose strange and eventful history is recorded in the following pages.

His companion and colleague, Julius Payer, was born at Schönau in Teplitz, Bohemia, in 1841, and received his education as a soldier at the Wiener-Neustadt Military Academy, 1856-59, where General Sonnklar was his teacher in geographical science, and early imbued his mind with a love for the grandeurs of the glacier world. With the rank of "Ober-Lieutenant" he served in the campaign of 1866 in Italy, and was *decorated* for his distinguished services at the battle of Custozza. Afterwards, while serving with his regiment in Tyrol, he gained great celebrity as one of the most successful Alpine climbers, and turned his experience as a mountaineer to profit in his surveys of the Orteler Alps and glaciers. Payer gained his first experience as an Arctic discoverer in the second German North Polar Expedition, under Koldeway and Hegemann—June 15, 1869—Sept. 11, 1870. His services during that expedition were of a most distinguished character. He shared in the most important discoveries which were then made, specially those of König Wilhelm's Land, and of the noble Franz-Josef Fjord. He acquired in East Greenland the experience of sledging, which was of such eminent use in his explorations of the great discovery of the *Tegetthoff* Expedition—Kaiser Franz-Joseph Land. He shines too as an author in his descriptions of Greenland scenes, in the *Second German North Polar Voyage*, published in 1874 by Brockhaus of Leipzig, and partially reproduced in an English translation by the Rev. L. Mercier and Mr. H. W. Bates. For these services, on the return of the expedition, he was again *decorated*, receiving the order of the Iron Crown.

In the voyage of the *Isbjörn*, June 21—Oct. 4, 1871,

we find him associated with Weyprecht in the pioneering voyage described in the first volume of this work, and lastly as joint commander of the renowned *Tegetthoff* expedition, June, 1872—September, 1874.

The Gold Medals entrusted to the Royal Geographical Society were awarded in 1875 : the Founder's Medal to Lieutenant Weyprecht, and the Patron's Medal to Lieutenant Julius Payer.

As these pages are passing through the Press, the country has been deeply moved by the unexpected intelligence of the return of the Arctic Expedition. Gratulations on its safe and happy return have been unanimously and eagerly expressed by all the organs of public opinion. Disappointment, however, has, we fear, fallen on many minds as, after the first feelings of joy at the safe arrival of the officers and crews of the *Alert* and *Discovery*, they read the brief telegraphic summary sent by Captain Nares : " Pole impracticable,"—" No land to northward." Popular enthusiasm looked rather for the conquest of the Pole; expected, perhaps, to read, one day, that the Union Jack had been hoisted there, to commemorate the triumph of England's perseverance at last rewarded. Few, we apprehend, would pass through the chill of these two clauses of the message to mark the hope contained in the third— " voyage otherwise successful."

In what special respects the success proclaimed was achieved, we must patiently wait for a future record to reveal; but while awaiting the history which no doubt will be written to justify and prove this announcement, let us exercise our loyal belief in the skill and courage of our countrymen, and feel persuaded, that what men could do under their circumstances no doubt was done by them.

The interest which will be excited afresh in Arctic discovery and adventure, will doubtless sharpen the interest in the volumes which record the fortunes of the Austrian expedition: and we venture to affirm—without undue partiality—that, though the history of Arctic exploration and discovery abounds in records of lofty resolution and patient endurance of almost incredible hardships, the narrative of the voyage of the *Tegetthoff* will be found to fall below none in these high qualities. The mere destiny of the vessel itself equals, if it does not exceed, in the element of the marvellous, anything which has before been recorded. Surely this is borne out when we think, that on August 20, 1872, the *Tegetthoff* was beset off the coast of Novaya Zemlya; remained a fast prisoner in the ice, spite of all the efforts made by her officers and crew to release her; drifted during the autumn and the terrible winter of 1872—amid profound darkness—whither they knew not: drifted to the 30th of August in the following year (1873), till, as if by magic, the mists lifted, and lo! a high, bold, rocky coast—lat. 79° 43′ E., long. 59° 33′—loomed out of the fog straight ahead of them. Close to this land—which could be visited with safety only twice, on the 1st and 3rd of the November of that year—the ship remained still fast bound in the ice. Not till the winter of 1873 had passed, and the sun had again returned, was it possible to explore the land, which had been so marvellously discovered. On the 10th of March, 1874, the sledge journeys commenced, and terminated May 3rd, after 450 miles had been passed over, and the surveys and explorations completed, which enabled Payer to write the description of Kaiser Franz-Josef Land, (vol. ii. pp. 476-496), which shows that other still. undefined lands, with an archipelago of islands, have been added to the geography of the earth.

But the perils of the expedition did not end here. On the 20th of August, 1874, it was resolved to abandon the *Tegetthoff* in the ice, and to return in sledges and boats to Europe. Captain Nares tells us, in his telegraphic despatch, that the sledging parties of the *Alert* and *Discovery* compassed on an average one-and-a-quarter mile per day on the terrible "Sea of Ancient Ice," and discovered, after the experience gained in seventy miles passed under these conditions, that the "Pole was impracticable." If our readers wish to have a conception of the toils and perils of the Austrian sledge parties on their return from the *Tegetthoff*, let them mark the single image presented to the mind by the statement (p. 245, vol. ii) :—" After the lapse of two months of indescribable efforts, the distance between us and the ship was not more than two German miles." Had the ice on the Novaya Zemlya seas remained as obstinate as it seems to have done in the new desolation, the "Sea of Ancient Ice," escape would have been as impossible to the *Tegetthoff's* crew, as advance towards the Pole was to the sledge parties of our last Arctic expedition. But fortunately soon after, "leads" opened out in the ice; the boats were launched, and after about another month of alternate rowing and sledging, the ice barrier was happily reached in the unusually high latitude 77° 40′; and the brave men who three months before had left the *Tegetthoff* were saved.

This is perhaps the most marked analogy between the perils of the two expeditions ; so far as those of our own are yet known. But the scientific conclusions of Lieutenant Payer, as set forth in the general Introduction to his narrative, strikingly harmonize with the actual discoveries of the *Alert* and *Discovery*. Already it is authoritatively announced, that there is no open Polar Sea : that this hypothesis is as baseless as the existence of

President's Land. In the fourth chapter of that Introduction (vol. i. pp. 42–53), our author has analyzed with great sagacity the various theories on which that hypothesis was made to rest, working up to the conclusion, that no such sea exists. The demonstration of experience now takes the place of enlightened argument and opinion; fact and theory are here at one.

Nor can we forbear to direct attention to another statement in the same chapter. Let our readers mark the prophetic spirit of the following passage: "All the changes and phenomena of this mighty network lead us to infer the existence of frozen seas up to the Pole itself; and according to my own experience, gained in three expeditions, I consider that the states of the ice between 82° and 90° N.L. will not essentially differ from those which have been observed south of latitude 82°; I incline rather to the belief that they will be found worse instead of better" (p. 51). And "worse instead of better" they have been found, as we cannot doubt, when we weigh the ominous significance of the designation the "Sea of Ancient Ice."

History may or may not verify the position which the telegram so briefly resumes—"The Pole impracticable." Impracticable no doubt it was, if the condition of the ice seen by our expedition in that awful sea be its normal condition. All that it was possible for men to dare and achieve, England will feel that her officers and sailors dared and achieved under the circumstances they encountered. It may be, that later experience will show, that even that Sea may present to future explorers an aspect less tremendous; yea, that in some seasons, which science may yet predict, when her theories of the sun-spots are matured and formulated, open water will be found, as perhaps it was found in the year of the expedition of the *Polaris*, where the heroic sledging parties from the *Alert* and *Discovery* saw nothing and found nothing, but piled-up barriers of ice rising to the height of 150 feet.

It would be idle to predict, in the face of these results, that the Pole shall yet be reached. Any confident prediction in this spirit would, at the present moment, be singularly inopportune, as well as unwise. But despair would be equally unjustifiable, while its influence would be most hurtful and depressing, especially if Arctic exploration and the attainment of the Pole were supposed to be identical propositions. There are two things: reaching the North Pole, and the exploration of the Polar region. If the former appeals more to the imagination, and readily calls forth the emotions which are fed by the love of the marvellous, the latter enlists the sympathies of those who take a broader view of the necessities of Arctic exploration.

These have found a powerful representative in one whose services entitle him to speak with authority, in the naval chief of the *Tegetthoff* expedition. At a meeting of the German Scientific and Medical Association held at Gratz in September of 1875, Weyprecht read a paper on the principles of Arctic exploration, in which, according to the summary of its contents, which appeared in *Nature*, October 11, 1875, he maintains, that the Polar regions offer, in certain important respects, greater advantages than any other part of the globe for the observation of natural phenomena—Magnetism, the Aurora, Meteorology, Geology, Zoology, and Botany. He deplores, that while large sums have been spent and much hardship endured for geographical knowledge, strictly scientific observations have been regarded as holding a secondary place. Though not denying the importance of geographical discovery, he maintains, that the main purpose of future Arctic expeditions should be the extension of our knowledge of the various natural phenomena which may be studied with so great advantage in those regions. He insists in that paper on the following propositions:—"1. Arctic exploration is of the highest importance to a knowledge of the laws of nature. 2. Geographical discovery in those regions is of superior importance only in so far as it extends the field of scientific investigation in its strict sense. 3. Minute

Arctic topography is of secondary importance. 4. The geographical Pole has for science no greater significance than any other point in high latitude. 5. Observation stations should be selected without reference to the latitude, but for the advantages they offer for the investigation of the phenomena to be studied. 6. Interrupted series of observations have only a relative value." The suggestions thrown out by Lieutenant Weyprecht have been taken up by one whose mind seems to rise instinctively to all high aims and objects. Prince Bismarck forthwith appointed a German Commission of Arctic Exploration, consisting of some of the most eminent men of science of whom Germany can boast, who reported to the Bundesrath in a memoir, the recommendations of which were unanimously adopted. From *Nature*, November 11, 1875, which we have already quoted, we borrow the following *résumé* of that report :—

"1. The exploration of the Arctic regions is of great importance for all branches of science. The Commission recommends for such exploration the establishment of fixed observing stations. From the principal station, and supported by it, exploring expeditions are to be made by sea and by land.

"The Commission is of opinion that the region to be explored by organised German Arctic explorers is the great inlet to the higher Arctic regions situated between the eastern shore of Greenland and the western shore of Spitzbergen.

* * * *

"3. It appears desirable, and, so far as scientific preparations are concerned, possible, to commence these Arctic expeditions in 1877.

"4. The Commission is convinced that an exploration of the Arctic regions, based on such principles, will furnish valuable results, even if limited to the region between Greenland and Spitzbergen; but it is also of opinion, that an exhaustive solution of the problems to be solved can only be expected when exploration is extended over the whole Arctic zone, and when other countries take their share in the undertaking.

"The Commission recommends, therefore, that the principles adopted for the German undertaking be commended to the governments of the states which take interest in Arctic inquiry, in order to establish, if possible, a complete circle of observing stations in the Arctic zones."

Thus we are brought face to face with two different purposes, which may be termed, respectively, the romantic and the scientific purposes of Arctic discovery. To the former the attainment of the Pole has hitherto been the all in all of a geographical discovery. "The Pole impracticable," telegraphed by Captain Nares, as the result of the expedition which has returned baffled to our shores, is a stern reproof to all, who would still advocate a dash at the Pole as the worthiest purpose of Arctic discovery. Aims and endeavours not so glaring, nor appealing in the same degree to the love of the marvellous, are suggested in the sagacious proposals of Lieutenant Weyprecht, to whom science will not refuse her calmer and more measured respect, and in whom, as Captain of the *Tegetthoff*, all who love deeds of daring and energy will find a congenial spirit.

To Lieutenant Payer has fallen the distinguished honour of being not only the colleague in command and friend of Weyprecht, but the historian of their common sufferings and common glory in an enterprise, the fame of which the world, we believe, will not willingly let die.

CONTENTS TO VOLUME I.

INTRODUCTION.

CHAPTER I.

THE FROZEN OCEAN . . . . *page* 3—19

1. The ice-sheet of the Arctic region.—2. "Leads" and "ice-holes" defined.—3. Pack-ice and drift-ice.—4, 5, 6. Various designations of ice-forms.—7. Estimate of the thickness of ice.—8. Rate of its formation.—9. Old ice.—10, 11. Characteristics of young ice.—12. Results of the unrest in Arctic seas.—13. The snow-sheet described.—14. Colour of field-ice.—15. Characteristics of sea-ice.—16. Specific gravity of ice.—17. Irregularity of the forms of ice.—18. Temperature of the Arctic Sea.—19. Noise caused by disruption.—20. The ice-blink.—21. The water-sky.—22. Evaporation.—23. Calmness of the sea beneath the ice.—24. Overturning of icebergs.—25. Change of the sea's colour near ice.—26. Icebergs described.—27. Noise caused by the overturning of icebergs.

CHAPTER II.

NAVIGATION IN THE FROZEN OCEAN . . . . *page* 19—34

1. Preparatory study necessary for Polar navigators.—2. Choice of a favourable year necessary.—3. Navigation in coast-water recommended.—4. Failure often caused by leaving the coast-water.—5. Distance possible to accomplish in one summer.—6. The best time of year.—7. Steam-power recommended.—8. The rate of speed.—9. The build of Arctic ships.—10. Tactics of a ship in the ice.—11. Small vessels preferred.—12. Iron ships not suitable.—13. Two vessels to be employed.—14. "Besetment" and how to avoid it.—15. The use of a balloon recommended.—16. The "crow's-nest."—17. Winds and calms.—18. A winter harbour or "dock."

CHAPTER III.

THE PENETRATION OF THE REGIONS WITHIN THE POLAR CIRCLE; THE PERIOD OF THE NORTH-WEST AND NORTH-EAST PASSAGES . *page* 34—42

1. The Pole.—2. Old fancy of reaching India through the ice.—3, 4, 5. The first Polar navigators.—6-10. The North-West and North-East Passages—11. Strange tales of the old discoverers.—12. The Polar world becomes the object of scientific investigation.—13. M'Clintock perfects the art of sledging.

CHAPTER IV.

THE INNER POLAR SEA . . . . *page* 42—53

1. The Arctic Sea compared to the glaciers of the Alps.—2, 3. Old fancies respecting an inner Polar Sea.—4. Improbability of such a sea existing.—5. Influence of the Gulf Stream.—6. The Polynjii seen by Wrangel.—7. State of the ice in different years as found by various expeditions.—8. Probability that the most northerly regions do not differ from those already discovered.—9. Improbability that the Pole can be reached by a ship.—10. The English expedition to penetrate Smith's Sound.

CHAPTER V.

THE FUTURE OF THE POLAR QUESTION . . . . *page* 53—62

1. Material advantage from Arctic voyages.—2. The commercial value of the North-west and North-east passages no longer thought of.—3. The Polar question a problem of science.—4. The increase of the safety and convenience with which the ice-navigation is now performed.—5. The means of conducting Polar expeditions perfected.—6. Sledge expeditions afford the chief hope of success.—7. Not much more to be expected from ships.—8. The route by Smith's Sound recommended.—9. The English expedition.—10. Lieut. Weyprecht's plan for united scientific investigation.

CHAPTER VI.

POLAR EQUIPMENTS . . . . *page* 62—81

1. Past experience to be consulted.—2. The commander.—3. Selection of the crew.—4. Discipline and pay.—5. The best men to be obtained.—6. Special qualifications.—7. The medical man.—8. An artist or photographer desirable.—9. Old ideas of equipment.—10. The greatest possible comfort necessary.—11. A table of the sizes of the vessels in various expeditions.—12. The

CONTENTS.   xxv

best kind of ships.—13. The allowance of food.—14. Spirituous liquors. -
15. The ship becomes a house in the winter.—16. The quarters of the men.
—17. Lamps and candles.—18. Clothing of the crew.—19. Instruments and
ammunition.—20. The cost of different expeditions.

THE PIONEER VOYAGE OF THE ISBJÖRN . . . . *page* 81—116

1. A pioneer expedition resolved on.—2. and 3. Route to the east of Spitzbergen.
—4. The *Isbjörn* chartered for the service.—5. Attempts to gain information
on the probable state of the ice.—6. An unfavourable ice year predicted.—
7. The expedition leaves Tromsoe.—8. The coast of Norway described.—
9. The *Isbjörn* in the ice. 10. Seeking a harbour.—11. Cape Look-out.—
12. Two ships met with.—13. In the ice. –14. The return to the ice-barrier.
15. The geological-formation of the western coast.—16. Arrive at Hope
Island.--17. Ice disappeared.—18. Whales abound —19. Splendid effects of
colour.—20. In a sea. -21. A run along the west coast of Novaya Zemlya.—
22. Storms compel us to keep to sea.—23. Object of the voyage.—24. The
Austro-Hungarian expedition of 1872.—25. The plan of the Austro-Hungarian
expedition.

VOYAGE OF THE "TEGETTHOFF."

CHAPTER I.

FROM BREMERHAVEN TO TROMSOE . . . . *page* 119—127

1. The qualities requisite for a Polar navigator.—2. The crew of the *Tegetthoff.*—
3. The *Tegetthoff* lifts her anchor.—4. The vessel.—5. Crossing the sea.—
6. The languages spoken on board the *Tegetthoff.*—7. The officers and crew of
the *Tegetthoff.*—8. Arrive at Tromsoe.—9. The first and last voyage of the
Tegetthoff begins.

CHAPTER II.

ON THE FROZEN OCEAN . . . . *page* 127—151

1. Within the frozen ocean.—2. The sea of Novaya Zemlya.—3. We continue
our course by steam.—4. The decay of ice.—5. Effects of light.—6. We
meet the *Isbjörn.*—8-10. The Barentz Islands described by Professor
Höfer.—11. Preparations for future contests with the ice.—12. Inclosed in
the land ice.—13. We celebrate the birthday of Francis Joseph I.—14. Our
prospects do not improve.—15. The *Tegetthoff* finally beset.

CHAPTER III.

DRIFTING IN THE NOVAYA ZEMLYA SEAS . . . . . . *page* 151—162

1. Winter begins.—2. The impossibility of reaching the coast of Siberia.—3. Unsuccessful efforts to get free.—4. The name-day of the Emperor Francis Joseph I.—5. Encounters with polar bears.—6. A " snow-finch" visits the ship.—7. Novaya Zemlya recedes gradually from our gaze.

CHAPTER IV.

THE "TEGETTHOFF" FAST BESET IN THE ICE . . . . . *page* 162—183

1. Signs indicate the insecurity of our position.—2. A dreadful Sunday.—3. We make ready to abandon the ship.—4. The dogs.—5. We return to the ship.—6. We drift in the Frozen Sea.—7. Our alarms.—8. Our constant state of readiness to meet destruction.

CHAPTER V.

OUR FIRST WINTER (1872) IN THE ICE . . . . . . *page* 183—202

1. Surrounded by deep twilight.—2. Our preparations for winter.—3. The difficulty of sledge-travelling.—4. Sumbu mistaken for a fox.—5. The rending of the ice.—6. Our short expeditions.—7. The continual threatening of the ice.—8. A bear shot.—9. The effect of the long Polar night.—10. The middle of the long night.—11. Christmas feasts.—12. The first hour of the new year.—13. The dogs allowed in the cabin.—14. Carlsen writes in the log-book.

CHAPTER VI.

LIFE ON BOARD THE "TEGETTHOFF" . . . . *page* 202—222

1. The *Tegetthoff* covered with snow.—2. The excessive condensation of moisture.—3. The destruction of the snow wall.—4. The removal of the tent roof.—5. The stove of Meidinger of Carlsruhe.—6. The arrangements of the officers' mess-room.—7. Those who occupied the mess-room.—8. Our meals.—9. Divine Service on deck.—10. After dinner.—11. The monotony of our life.—12. After supper.—13. Middendorf contrasting the influence of climate on men.—14. Our sanitary condition.—15. Baths.—16. Passages from my journal.—17. A school instituted.

CHAPTER VII.

ICE PRESSURES . . . . page 222—227

1. Preparations for leaving the ship.—2. Extracts from journal.

CHAPTER VIII.

THE WANE OF THE LONG POLAR NIGHT . . . . . page 227—237

1. The light increases.—2. A bear hunt.—3. Table of the course of the *Tegetthoff*.—4. Throw out bottles inclosing an account of the events of the expedition.

CHAPTER IX.

THE RETURN OF LIGHT.—THE SPRING OF 1873 . . . page 237—258

1. The sunrise.—2. Our first look at each other.—3. Visits from bears.—4. The carnival.—5. Continual fall of snow.—6. Return of birds.—7. Ill health of Dr. Kepes.—8. Bear shot.—9. A road constructed.—10. Reading without artificial light.—11. Accumulation of rubbish round the ship.—12. Begin to dig out the ship.—13. Surprised by bears.—14. Our hopes to reach Siberia.—15. Snow continues to fall.—16. Visited by birds. 17. The steam machinery put in working order.—18. A partial eclipse of the Sun.—19. Birth o four Newfoundland puppies.

CHAPTER X.

THE SUMMER OF 1873 . . . . page 258—275

1. Decay of the walls of ice.—2. The blaze of light on clear days.—3. Our constant digging.—4. Continual sinking of the ship.—5. Nothing but ice. —6. Short expeditions.—7. Feast on the birthday of the Emperor.—8. Table showing our change of place.—9. Some paragraphs from the Admiral's report of the *Tegetthoff*.—10. Sounding the depth of the sea.

CHAPTER XI.

NEW LANDS . . . . page 275—283

1. Seal-hunting.—2. Sunset at midnight.—3. The second summer gone. 4. Land at last.—5. Kaiser Franz-Josef's Land.—6. Hochstetter island.

CHAPTER XII.

THE AUTUMN OF 1873.—THE STRANGE LAND VISITED . . *page* 283—294

1. Autumn of 1873.—2. Resolve to abandon the vessel.—3. Daylight begins to fail.—4. Everything in readiness to leave the ship.—5. Wilczek Island.—6. Our joy at reaching land.—7. Exploring the island.—8. An expedition.—9. The silence of Arctic Regions.—10. The island continues a mystery.

CHAPTER XIII.

OUR SECOND WINTER IN THE ICE . . . . *page* 294—318

1. Night begins to reign.—2. Leisure for study.—3. Complete darkness.—4. Continual fall of snow.—5. The middle of the second Polar night.—6. Ill temper of the dogs.—7. The dogs.—8. Pekel, Sumbu, and Jubinal.—9. Christmas time.—10.—Our life in the ship.—11. Improvement in health.—12. Scurvy.

CHAPTER XIV.

SUNRISE OF 1874 . . . . *page* 318—322

1. Return of the moon.—2. Sun appears above the horizon.—3. Lieutenant Weyprecht and I resolve to abandon the ship after the sleigh journeys.

CHAPTER XV.

THE AURORA . . . . *page* 322—335

1. The northern lights.—2—4. The appearance of the aurora.—5. The influence on the magnetic needle.—6. Description of the aurora by Lieutenant Weyprecht.

LIST OF ILLUSTRATIONS.

TWILIGHT AT MIDDAY—FEBRUARY, 1874	*Frontispiece.*

	PAGE
THE FIRST ICE . . .	89
STILL LIFE IN THE FROZEN OCEAN .	129
GWOSDAREW INLET . . .	137
FORMATION OF THE DEPOT AT "THE THREE COFFINS"	146
THE "TEGETTHOFF" AND "ISBJÖRN" SEPARATE	147
THE "TEGETTHOFF" FINALLY BESET	149
ATTEMPTS TO GET FREE IN SEPTEMBER .	153
SEAL-HUNTING—SEPTEMBER, 1872	155
SHOOTING AT A TARGET—OCTOBER, 1872 .	157
PARHELIA ON THE COAST OF NOVAYA ZEMLYA	160

LIST OF ILLUSTRATIONS.

	PAGE
AN OCTOBER NIGHT IN THE ICE	169
THE MOON WITH ITS HALO	175
OUR COAL HOUSE ON THE FLOE	179
THE TWILIGHT IN NOVEMBER, 1872	184
SUMBU CHASED FOR A FOX	186
WANDERINGS ON THE ICE IN OUR FIRST WINTER	188
ENCOUNTER WITH A POLAR BEAR	192
ICE HOLE COVERED WITH YOUNG ICE	193
CARLSEN MAKES THE ENTRY IN THE LOG	200
THE "TEGETTHOFF" IN THE FULL MOON	203
DIVINE SERVICE ON DECK	211
ICE PRESSURE IN THE POLAR NIGHT	223
FRUITLESS ATTEMPT TO RESCUE MATOSCHKIN	231
SUNRISE, 1873	239
THE CARNIVAL ON THE ICE	243

	PAGE
THE "TEGETTHOFF" DRIFTING IN PACK-ICE.—MARCH, 1873	247
SOUNDING IN THE FROZEN OCEAN	273
APPROACHING THE LAND BY MOONLIGHT	291
DEPARTURE OF THE SUN IN THE SECOND WINTER	297
NOON ON DECEMBER 21, 1873 .	303
PEKEL, SUMBU, AND JUBINAL	307
IN THE MESS-ROOM	312
THE AURORA DURING THE ICE PRESSURE	325

ERRATA.

Page 31, note, *for* " geographical " *read* " German."
Page 268, *for* " shi " *read* " ship in."

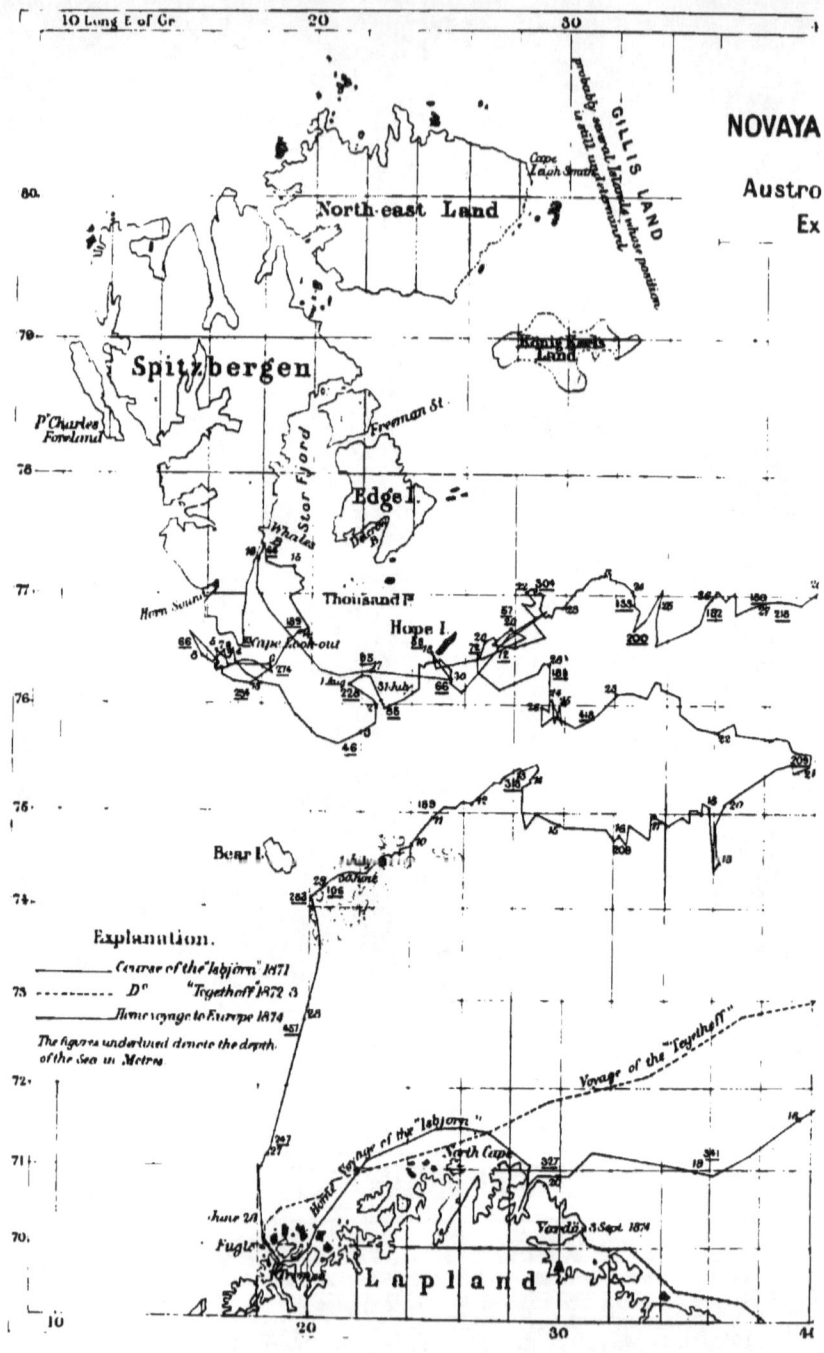

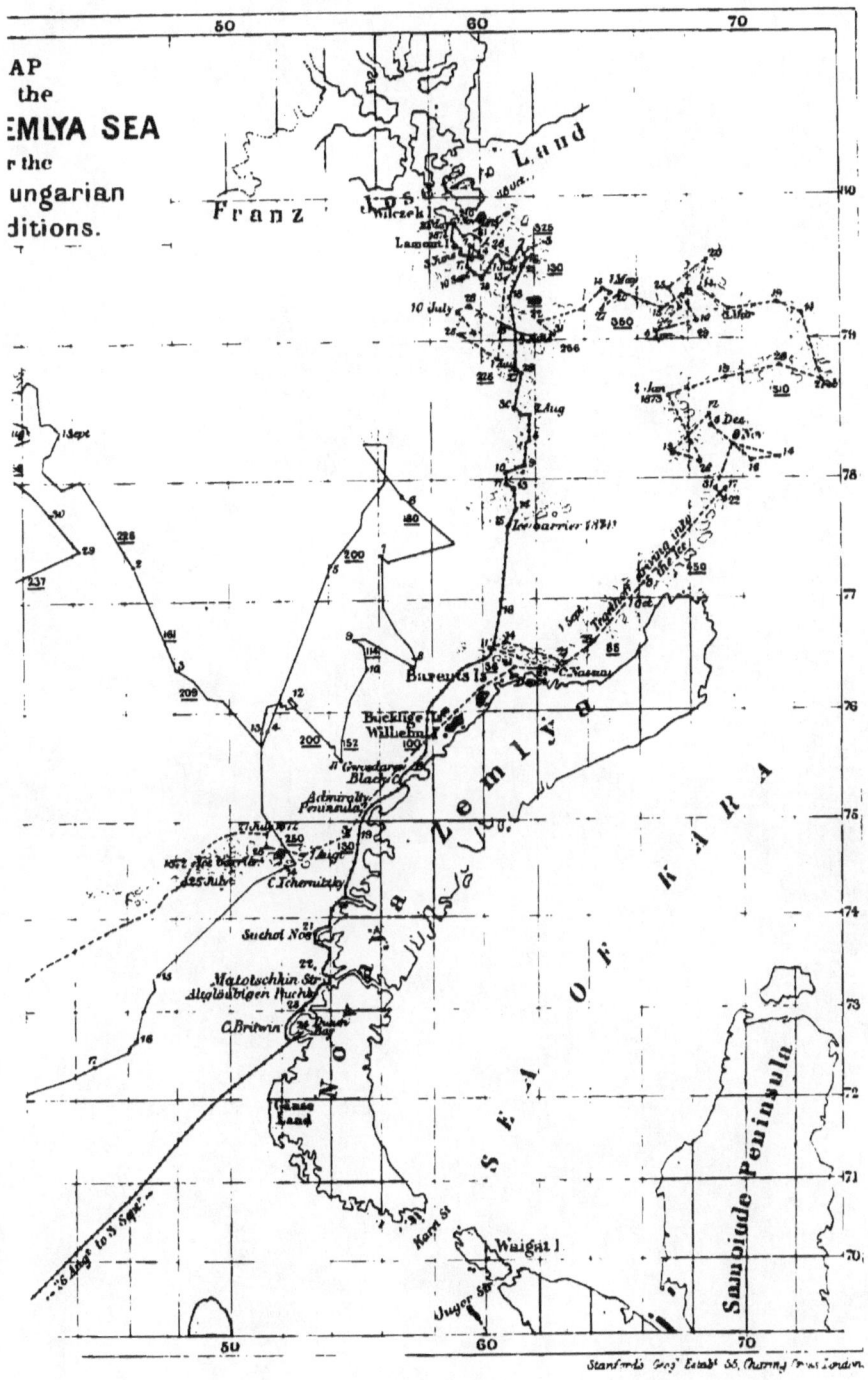

INTRODUCTION.

AUSTRIAN ARCTIC VOYAGES.

INTRODUCTION.

CHAPTER I.

THE FROZEN OCEAN.

1. THE ice-sheet spread over the Arctic region is the effect and sign of the low temperature which prevails within it. During nine or ten months of the year this congealing force continues to act, and if the frozen mass were not broken up by the effects of sun and wind, of rain, waves, and currents, and by the rents produced in it from the sudden increase of cold, the result would necessarily be an absolutely impenetrable covering of ice. The parts of this enormous envelope of ice sundered by these various causes now become capable of movement, and are widely dispersed in the form of ice-fields and floes.

2. The water-ways which separate these parts are called "leads," or, when their extent is considerable, "ice-holes." The meshes of this vast net, which is constantly in motion, open and close under the action of winds and currents in summer; and it is only in its southern parts that the action of waves, rain, and thaw produces any considerable detachments. Towards the end of autumn, the ice, forming anew, consolidates the interior portions, while its outer edge pushes forward, like the end of a glacier, into lower regions, until about the end of February the culminating point of congelation is attained. Motionless adhesion of the fields, which naturally reach their greatest size in winter, does not, however, exist even then; for during this period they are incessantly exposed to displacement and pressure from the currents of the sea and the air.

3. When the ice is more or less closed, so as to render navigation impossible, it is called "pack-ice," and "drift-ice," when it appears in detached pieces amid predominating water. Since there are forces operating which promote the loosening process at its outer edge, and its consolidation within, it is self-evident, that the interior portions tend to the character of "pack-ice," and its outer margin to that of "drift-ice." This general rule, however, is so modified in many places, by local causes,

currents, and winds, that we find not unfrequently at the outer margin of the ice thick barriers of pack-ice, and in the inner ice, ice-holes (polynia[1]) and drift-ice.

4. Ice navigation, during its course of three hundred years, has created a number of terms to designate the external forms of ice, the meaning of which must be clearly defined. Ice formed from salt-water is called "field-ice;" that from the waters of rivers and lakes "sweet-water ice." The latter is as hard as iron, and so transparent that it is scarcely to be distinguished from water. Icebergs are masses detached from glaciers. The words "patch," "floe," "field," express relative magnitude, descriptive of the smallest ice-table up to the ice-field of many miles in diameter. The term "floe," however, is generally applied to every kind of field-ice, without reference to its size. The ice which lies along coasts, or which adheres to a group of islands within a sound, is called "land ice." Sledge expeditions depend on its existence and character. Along the coast-edge land ice is broken by the waves and tide, and the forms of its upheaval and deposition on the shore constitute the so called "ice-foot." Broken ice, or "brash," is an accumulation of the smaller fragments of ice which are found only on the extreme edge of the ice-belt.

[1] *Polynia*, a Russian term for an open water space.—Glossary in Kane's *Arctic Explorations*, vol. i., p. 14.

"Bay-ice" is ice, of recent formation and its vertical depth is inconsiderable.

5. Land-ice is less exposed to powerful disturbances, and its surface, therefore, is comparatively level, and is only here and there traversed by small hillocks called "hummocks" or "torrosy." These are the results of former pressures, and they are gradually reduced to the common level by evaporation, by thawing, and by the snow drifting over them.

6. But ice-floes exposed to constant motion from winds and currents, and to reciprocal pressure, have a more or less undulating character. On these are found piles of ice heaped one upon another, rising to a height of twenty or even fifty feet, alternating with depressions, which collect the thawed water in clear ice-lakes during the few weeks of summer in which the temperature rises above the freezing point. The specific gravity of this water, where it does not communicate with the sea by cracks, is in all cases the same with the specific gravity of pure sweet water; and as the salt is gradually eliminated from the ice, the water produced is perfectly drinkable. In the East Greenland Sea ice-floes frequently measure more than twelve nautical miles across—these are ice-fields properly so called.[1] In the

[1] Ice-fields have been seen there equal to the superficial extent of a German principality, or even to the Duchy of Salzburg.

Spitzbergen and Novaya Zemlya Seas, they are much smaller, as Parry also found.

7. The thickness which ice acquires in the course of a winter, when its formation is not disturbed, is about eight feet. In the Gulf of Boothia, Sir John Ross found the greatest thickness about the end of May; it was then ten feet on the sea and eleven feet on the lakes. In his winter harbour in Melville Island, Parry met with ice seven or seven-and-a-half feet thick; and Wrangel gives the thickness of a floe on the Siberian coast, which had been formed in the course of a winter, at nine-and-a-half feet. According to the observations of Hayes the ice measured nine feet two inches in thickness in Port Foulke. He estimates it, however, by implication, far higher in Smith's Sound : " I have never seen," he says, "an ice-table formed by direct freezing which exceeded the depth of eighteen feet."

8. The rate at which ice is formed decreases as the thickness of the floe increases, and it ceases to be formed as soon as the floe becomes a non-conductor of the temperature of the air by the increase of its mass, or when the driving of the ice-tables one over the other, or the enormous and constantly accumulating covering of snow, places limits to the penetration of the cold.

9. While therefore the thickness which ice in free

formation attains is comparatively small, fields of ice from thirty to forty feet high are met with in the Arctic Seas; but these are the result of the forcing of ice-tables one over the other by pressure, and are designated by the name of "old ice," which differs from young ice by its greater density, and has a still greater affinity with the ice of the glacier when it exhibits coloured veins.

10. When the cold is excessive a sheet of ice several inches thick is formed on open water in a few hours; this, however, is not pure ice, but contains a considerable amount of sea-salt not yet eliminated; complete elimination of the saline matter takes place only after continuous additions of ice to its under surface. A newly-formed sheet of ice is flexible like leather, and as it becomes harder by the continued cold, its saline contents come to the surface in a white frosty efflorescence.

11. Hayes mentions that he met with fields of ice from twenty to a hundred feet thick in Smith's Sound. But if it is difficult in many cases to distinguish glacier-ice, when found in small fragments, from detached portions of field-ice, it is often still more difficult to distinguish between old and new ice, and the attempt to do so is merely arbitrary, because their masses depend not on their age alone, but on other processes to which they are exposed. A floe of normal thickness is never more

than two or three years old; and if it is to exist and preserve its size for a longer period, it must somewhere attach itself to land-ice, so as to escape destruction from mechanical causes, and dissolution from drifting southwards. Many floes run their course from freezing to melting within a year.

12. The perpetual unrest in the Arctic Sea, which continues undiminished even in the severest winter, and the incessant change in the "leads" and "ice-holes," are the main causes of the increase of the ice, both in its area and in its vertical depth. Were this constant movement to cease, the result would be the formation of a sheet of ice of the uniform thickness of about eight feet over the whole Polar region.

13. A layer of snow, which, like the ice itself, is at a minimum in autumn, covers the whole surface of all the ice-fields. This snow, which in winter is sometimes as hard as a rock, sometimes as fine as dust, takes, towards the end of summer, more and more the character of the glacier snow of our lofty Alpine ranges. Its grains, in a humid state, exceed the size of beans, and when in motion they make a rustling noise like sand. This granular snow is the residuum of the incomplete evaporation of what fell in the winter, and of the surface of the ice which has become "rotten" and porous. Its crystals are frequently from a third to a

sixth of an inch in length, and firm ice is found even in autumn only at the depth of one or two feet. In the North of Spitzbergen, Parry observed that the surface of the ice was frequently cut up into ice-needles of more than a foot long by the drops of rain, which in summer fall upon it, and in some places he found it overspread with red snow. We ourselves never saw the phenomenon observed by Parry, and the ice-crystals we met with seldom exceeded the length given above.

14. Field-ice is of a delicate azure-blue colour, and of great density, and there is, in these respects, no difference between that of the Arctic and Antarctic regions. Cook, indeed, calls the South Polar ice colourless, though Sir James Clark Ross speaks expressly of the blueness of its ice-masses. Sea-ice surpasses the ice of the Alps both in the beauty of its colour and in its density. The glorious blue of the fissures is due to the incidence of light, the blue rays of which only are reflected, while the other rays are absorbed. A spectrum observation made in 1869 on a Greenland ice-field gave brownish red, yellow, green and blue. The yellowish spots observed in ice are due to the presence of innumerable microscopic animalculæ.

15. Sea-ice, which, when the cold is intense, is hard and brittle, loses this quality with the increase of tem-

perature till it acquires an incredible toughness, far exceeding that of glaciers; and floes several feet thick bend under mutual pressure before they split. Hence the fruitlessness, especially in summer, of all attempts to loosen the connexion of its parts by blasting with gunpowder.

16. The specific gravity of sea-ice is 0.91, and accordingly about nine parts of a cubical block of ice are under water, while one part only rises above the surface. If, however, the ice of a floe be irregularly formed and full of bubbles, the specific gravity will be correspondingly reduced, and the volume submerged may diminish to two-thirds of the whole mass.

17. The irregularity of the forms of ice is so great, that no deduction can safely be drawn from them; cases may occur where a recently-formed ice-floe, which has been attached to old ice, is forced by its neighbour to sink under the normal level; hence the submergence of floes beneath the level of the sea is often overstated.

18. The temperature of the Arctic Sea at the surface is generally below the freezing point, and then increases slightly with the depth. Sir James Ross observed that the temperature in all oceans does not alter at great depths, and placed this constant temperature at $3°$ R. In summer the temperature of the atmosphere rises

little above 0°, and, according to Sir James Ross, it is still less at the South Pole, because he saw no thaw-water streaming down from the icebergs there as he did in the North. It was first observed in Forster's days, that is about a century ago, that the salt was gradually eliminated from frozen sea-water. Of this fact Cook knew nothing; and even Sir James Ross endorses Davis's remark that "the deep sea freezes not." But the fact that ice is formed on the open sea, and far from the vicinity of land, was first asserted by Scoresby, and has been confirmed by all subsequent observers, though it was long disputed.

19. The crackling sound so commonly heard along the outer edge of the ice exposed to the action of the waves, is a consequence of the penetration of its pores by the sea-water, which is then immediately frozen, and disruption follows at once. But disruption on a far grander scale is due to a cause the very opposite of this, the sudden contraction and splitting of the ice, even in the great ice-fields, which is produced usually in winter by the sudden fall of the temperature.

20. When light falls on a field of pack-ice, it is reflected in the stratum of air above it, and this span of light, called the "ice-blink," just above the horizon, warns the navigator of the impossibility of penetrating

further. This phenomenon is often observed also over drift-ice, although not so intense nor so yellow in colour as over pack-ice.

21. Water spaces, on the other hand, show their presence by dark spots on the horizon, produced by the formation of clouds from ascending mists. These are the so called "water-sky," and faithfully indicate the "leads" beneath them. Above the larger "ice-holes," they assume the dark colours of a thunder-sky, though they are never so strongly defined.

22. The annual evaporation from the surface of the ice, which even in winter is never entirely interrupted during the severest frost, and the destruction of ice by the action of rain and waves are balanced, to speak generally, by its re-formation by frost. The maximum accumulation of ice takes place in spring, its minimum in the beginning of autumn. We observed in the autumn of 1873 not only the evaporation of the snow of the preceding winter, but also a vertical decrease of ice of about four feet. Evaporation is, therefore, the most potent regulator of the balance between waste and growth in the accumulation of ice; and next in importance is the drifting of its masses towards the south through all those openings by which the Polar waters mingle with the waters of lower latitudes.

23. However great the agitation of the sea may be in

the open ocean, and though it may dash its waves with wild fury on the edge of the ice, within the icy girdle it is undisturbed, in consequence of the enormous weight of the superincumbent masses. It is only in the large "ice-holes," and when the winds are very high, that the action of waves is discernible. An isolated accumulation of floes in a circular form, suffices to produce a calm interior sea, and its outer edge only encounters the beat of the ocean.

24. The ceaseless attack to which the ice is exposed on its outer edge is the cause of its excavation and undermining. Hence its centre of gravity is constantly displaced; and the overturning of its masses and its strange transformations are the consequences of this instability. The smaller the masses of the ice, the more fantastic are the shapes they assume.

25. Change of colour in the sea as we enter the ice-region is frequently, though not invariably, observed. Almost immediately on entering the ice, its normal dull green colour gives place to a deep ultramarine blue, especially in the East Greenland seas, and this colour is maintained under all changes of the weather, and is only modified by local currents. Two hundred and fifty years ago it appeared to Hudson, on the coast of Spitzbergen, that the sea, whenever it was free from ice, was green, and that its being covered with ice and its

blueness of colour were intimately connected. Sir James Ross states that in both Polar oceans the colour of the sea changes in the neighbourhood of ice, and that the dull brownish colour sometimes seen near pack-ice in the Antarctic Ocean is owing to an infinite number of animalculæ. The rapid fall of the temperature of the water to the zero point is another indication that ice is near.

26. Of all the ice-formations in the Arctic Seas, icebergs are the most enormous. "It is well-known that ice is not by any means so heavy as water, but readily floats upon its surface. Consequently whenever a glacier enters the sea, the dense salt water tends to buoy it up. But the great tenacity of the frozen mass enables it to resist the pressure for a time. By and by, however, as the glacier reaches deeper water, its cohesion is overcome, and large fragments are forced from its terminal front and floated up from the bed of the sea to sail away as icebergs."[1] This process is sometimes called "the calving" of the glaciers; and the direction of the cleavage is a pre-indication of the forms of the masses when detached. The characteristic features of icebergs are their simple outline, differing widely from the fantastic shapes which the fragments of sea-ice tend to assume; their great height as compared with their

[1] Geikie's *Great Ice Age*, pp. 38, 39.

breadth—their greenish-blue colour—their distinct stratification—their slight transparency—and the roughly-granulated character of their ice. Icebergs with long, sharp-pointed peaks, like those exhibited in numerous illustrations, have no real existence. It is only fragments of field-ice, raised up by pressure, exposed to the action of waves and the process of evaporation which are transformed into fantastic shapes. Icebergs are generally of a pyramidal or tabular shape, and in time they are usually rounded off into irregular cones. They vary in height from 20 to 300 feet. Sir John Ross (1818) mentions an iceberg of 51 feet; Baffin (1615) of 240 feet; Parry (1819) of 258 feet; Kane (1853) of 300 feet; and Hayes (1861) one 315 feet high, the depth of which below the water-line he estimated at half a mile. On the coast of East Greenland, Scoresby once counted 500 icebergs, some of which reached the height of 200 feet; and during the second German North-Pole expedition, we saw many at the mouth of the Kaiser Franz-Josef fiord which measured 220 feet in height. In Austria-Sound, and on the east coast of Kron-Prinz Rudolph's land, their altitude varied from 80 to 200 feet. From the covering of mist which envelops them, icebergs generally appear much higher than they really are, and their depth below the surface is not so considerable as is generally supposed. In an iceberg 200 feet above the water, a total height of 600 to 800 feet may, as a mean, be inferred. It is only glaciers of a very great size which shed icebergs; smaller glaciers, like those of Novaya Zemlya, only strew the sea with a multitude of fragments which resemble broken sea-ice. Hence the appearance of icebergs is connected with the proximity to glacier-covered lands, and with the currents which prevail along their coasts. Baffin's Bay, Smith's Sound, East Greenland, the South-East of Greenland, Austria Sound, are the principal places where they collect together and lie like fleets before the entrances of bays and gulfs. Undercurrents of the sea take them not unfrequently in directions contrary to the drift of the field-ice, which depends only on upper-currents; and abnormal winds may sometimes carry them out to seas where they have been seldom or never seen.[1] This appears to be the case even with those met with on the north-west coast of Novaya Zemlya. On the other hand, they have never been seen on the coasts of Siberia, which have no glaciers.

27. The constant displacement of the centre of gravity of an iceberg, resulting from the unsymmetrical decrease of its form, causes its periodical oversetting; and the

[1] In the North Atlantic Ocean down to 40° N. L.

different temperature of the internal and external ice is the principal cause of its rending asunder with a noise like thunder; a process which occurs generally in the height of summer.

CHAPTER II.

NAVIGATION IN THE FROZEN OCEAN.

1. ALTHOUGH it be impossible to give any one, who has not with his own eyes seen the Arctic Sea, a perfectly clear conception of its character, the phenomena described in the preceding chapter are sufficient to indicate the difficulties and dangers to which its navigation is necessarily exposed. And to these difficulties and dangers, formidable enough in themselves, are often added the evil influences of preconceived theories and exaggerated expectations, usually followed by bitter disillusions. The calm judgment, which, to all the bold plans of navigation within the Polar basin, opposes distrust in their feasibility, while it points to the hundred expeditions which have at last returned home after penetrating but a little way into the frozen sea, is an attainment of slow growth. Years, too, must be devoted to the theoretical study of the Polar question, to the examination of all that predecessors have

experienced and recorded. But this study is very important to polar navigators; for the discoveries which they too readily regard as exclusively their own prove sometimes to have been made centuries before them.

2. A most essential element of success is the choice of a favourable ice year; and the commander of an expedition must possess sufficient self-control to return, as soon as he becomes convinced of the existence of conditions unfavourable for navigation. It is better to repeat the same attempt on a second or even a third summer, than with conscious impotence to fight against the supremacy of the ice.

3. Polar navigators have learnt in the school of experience to distinguish between navigation in the frozen seas remote from the land, and navigation in the so-called coast-waters. The former is far more dangerous, entirely dependent on accident, exposed to grave catastrophes, and without any definite goal. It affords no certainty of finding a winter harbour for the long period when cold and darkness render navigation impossible. On the other hand, a strip of open water, which retreats before the growth of the land-ice only in winter, forms itself along coasts, and especially under the lee of those exposed to marine currents running parallel to them; and this coast-water does not arise from the thawing of the ice through the greater

heat of the land, but from the land being an immovable barrier against wind, and therefore against ice-currents. The inconstancy of the wind, however, may baffle all the calculations of navigation; for coast-water, open as far as the eye can reach, may be filled with ice in a short time by a change of the wind. Land-ice often remains on the coasts even during summer, and in this case there is nothing to be done but to find the open navigable water between the extreme edge of the fast-ice and the drift-ice. Should the drift become pack-ice, the moment must be awaited when winds setting in from the land carry off the masses of ice blocking the navigation, and open a passage free from ice, or at least only partially covered with drift-ice. It is evident that navigation in coast waters must be slow and gradual, though it has always been attended with the greatest advantages. Barentz was the first who tested its value; but it was Parry, the most distinguished of all Polar navigators, who discovered its full importance, and from his day it has been accepted as an incontrovertible canon of ice-navigation. On this point he himself says: "Our experience, I think, has clearly shown, that the navigation of the Polar Seas can never be performed with any degree of certainty without a continuity of land. It was only by watching the openings between the ice and the shore that our late progress to the westward was effected; and had the land continued in the desired direction, there can be no question, that we should have continued to advance, however slowly, towards the completion of our enterprise."[1]

4. The successes of the English in the North American Archipelago were the result of this mode of navigation. Its principle is to search for and sail along the network of narrow channels when the main passage is blocked by pack-ice, and to turn to account the narrowest opening between the ice and the land. In the Siberian coast expeditions also this method of constantly following the coast waters has been successfully observed. Where coast water does not exist, or only to a limited extent, as on the east coast of Greenland, this method is of course impracticable. The fate of the second German North Pole expedition is an illustration of this; it was ordered to penetrate in this direction, and its failure was inevitable. On the other hand, all the unsuccessful attempts of expeditions to penetrate northward from Spitzbergen—expeditions whose course and termination resemble each other as one egg resembles another—may be reckoned among those in seas remote from land. To the same category belong the

[1] Parry's *Journal of a Voyage for the Discovery of a North-west Passage*, 1819-20, p. 298. 4to. London, 1821.

expeditions for the discovery of a north-east passage, and simply because of the great extent of frozen sea between Novaya Zemlya and Cape Tcheljuskin.

5. In the frozen sea remote from the land, from 200 to 300, or at the most 400 nautical miles must, according to all past experience, be regarded as the greatest distance which a vessel is able to compass, under the most favourable conditions, during the few weeks of summer in which navigation is possible. The fact that Sir James Ross at the South Pole, and Norwegian fishermen in the Sea of Kara accomplished still greater distances, only proves that they were little or not at all impeded by ice. Ross observed that the ice-floes of the Southern Arctic Seas are smaller than those of the Northern: "The cause of this is explained by the circumstance of the ice of the southern regions being so much more exposed to violent agitations of the ocean, whereas the northern sea is one of comparative tranquillity."[1] The rarer occurrence of land at the South Pole permits freer scope to the currents of the sea, diminishes the opportunity for the growth of ice on the coasts, tends to widen the passages in the network of water-ways, and thus facilitates navigation. Even the swell of the sea within the ice is observed in the South Polar Ocean, while it is never seen in the North. Besides the greater

[1] Sir J. C. Ross's *Southern Antarctic Voyage*, vol. ii., p. 151.

hindrances peculiar to the whole North Polar Sea, there is the specially unfavourable circumstance, in the case of the North-East passage, that the shallowness of the Siberian Sea prevents a close navigation of its coasts.

6. The choice of the most appropriate season is another important consideration in ice-navigation; for this period does not fall at the same time in all seas, and the disregard of season was a common cause of the failures of the expeditions of earlier centuries. Since the frozen sea remains unbroken and almost unaffected by the action of the sun even in June, and at that time extends far to the south, it is evident that all attempts to force a passage in that month are labour thrown away. The ice-barrier retreating northward, or the transformation of pack into drift ice, leaves free navigable water four or five weeks later. The month of August is the best time for ice-navigation in Baffin's Bay; the end of July or beginning of August on the East Greenland coasts; the second half of August and the beginning of September in the Spitzbergen waters; and in the region of the Parry Islands the favourable opportunity ends about the beginning of September. In general it seems that the time most propitious for all the coast-water routes, begins some weeks earlier than the corresponding period in the frozen seas remote from land.

But since, even in the first weeks of September, the most promising conditions are often succeeded by a sudden reaction due to storms, to cold setting in rapidly, or to excessive falls of snow, navigation in the land-remote frozen seas, in itself so extremely hazardous, becomes specially critical, just when the ice-sheet at its minimum appears to promise the greatest results.

7. The help of steam power is an indispensable requisite, as by it a vessel is able to defy the capricious changes of the wind. The movements of a ship amid the ice are made in interminable curves, and the power to describe an arc with the least radius, enables a vessel to follow up narrow and often blocked water ways. As it is incessantly exposed to severe shocks from the ice, a paddle-wheel steamer is useless; and even in screw-steamers care must be taken to protect the propeller by a special construction.

8. The rate of speed of a vessel in the ice must necessarily be moderate. From three to six miles an hour are sufficient: and a rate of eight or ten miles would soon render her not seaworthy. But even with this reduced rate, her whole framework is shaken and loosened at last by the incessant shocks she sustains; and this condition of the ship becomes apparent when concussion with the ice is followed not by a noise as of thunder, but by a low, dull, groaning sound. The larger a vessel,

the less her capacity to withstand these shocks, and the sooner will these signs of her diminished strength betray themselves.

9. An Arctic ship should be built with sharp rather than with full lines, so that when pressed by the ice, she may more easily escape being nipped and crushed. A ship built with what is called—in England—full lines, a full, round ship, is not easily raised but is liable to be crushed by ice-pressure. The *Hansa* was built in this manner, and was crushed by the first squeeze from the ice; the *Germania* and the *Tegetthoff* were both of them sharp-built ships, and stood the test of the ice excellently well. To protect it from the effects of grinding on ragged "ice-tongues," the hull is generally iron-plated for some feet under water, and the bows are strengthened as much as possible, because this part of the ship is exposed to the greatest shocks.

10. The tactics of a ship in the ice are guided entirely by the character of the hindrances to be overcome. If the ice-fields be large and heavy, they are then generally separated by broader water-ways and "leads," and a ship may often amid such ice follow her course for hours with few deviations, subject always to the danger of being "beset" and crushed. When the passage is blocked by a barrier of ice, the situation becomes grave and serious; for such fields are not to be displaced by any

force which the ship may exert, and nothing is left to the navigator but to await their parting asunder in a position as sheltered as possible. When the ice is loose and the floes comparatively small, the impeding barriers may be charged by the ship. She may then force asunder some of these floes or separate them by the continuous pressure of steam-power. In cases of this kind, large vessels have the advantage and can bring to bear a greater amount of pressure, whereas smaller ones stick fast and remain immovable. These accumulations of ice, while they make a "besetment" more likely, diminish the danger of pressure.

11. Hence it is clear that small are to be preferred to large vessels for ice-navigation, except under circumstances of rare occurrence; first, because they are more readily handled, and next, because of their greater power of resistance and of their being more easily raised under pressure from the ice. Their one disadvantage of lesser momentum is of comparatively slight consequence. The experience of all the North Pole expeditions of this century shows, that ships of 150, or at the most of 300 tons, are best suited for all purposes.

12. Iron ships have often been employed, but with no success; they are far less able to bear pressure than wooden ships, as was proved, among other things, by

the fate of the *River Tay* in 1868, in Baffin's Bay, and of the *Sophia*, a Swedish ship of discovery in the north of Spitzbergen.

13. It admits of no question, that two vessels should be employed in preference to one, and this should be accepted as a first principle whenever the means at our disposal admit of it. Both ships should also be provided with steam power, for otherwise their separation is almost inevitable,—a danger, however, for which, under all circumstances, they must be prepared.

14. All that is commonly understood about piercing the ice by sawing and boring through it is a delusion, and arises from the misunderstanding of technical expressions. Where there is navigable water, there any one can sail—where there is none, no one. In 1869 and 1870, after coming on a *cul-de-sac* of ice in Greenland to the east of Shannon Island, we could not penetrate a yard further; in 1871, in loose, but solid ice, we drew away only by warping on the smaller floes, without being able to make the slightest progress, and in 1872 we were twice "beset," in heavy ice, in spite of our steam power. The penetration of close pack-ice is an impossibility: in this case patient endurance is alone of any avail, and hence Sir John Ross so emphatically recommends the Polar navigator "never to lose sight of the two words caution and

patience."[1] If a vessel, therefore, is arrested by impenetrable masses barring its way, the breaking up of the ice must be patiently awaited, and this, generally, is effected by calms, although the ebb and flow of the tide appear to have an influence on the solidity of the ice. It is then usual with sailing ships to seek the larger "ice-holes," or keep in the freest water-ways, in order to guard against the danger of being completely inclosed. These precautions, however, are not so requisite for steam-vessels, as their power to escape quickly and in any direction, secures them against this danger. A steam-vessel may even venture to fasten on to an ice-floe by means of an ice-anchor, and of course under its lee, the fires being banked up, so that by getting up steam she may shift her place as soon as the ice moves nearer. As a principle, and so far as it is possible without the exhaustion of her powers, a ship in the ice should endeavour to be in constant motion, even though this entail many changes of her course and the temporary return to a position which had been abandoned. The making fast to a floe, however, should never be attempted, except when every hope of navigating in the surrounding waters has been proved fruitless. The fastening a vessel to an iceberg diminishes, indeed, its drifting,

[1] Sir John Ross—*Second Voyage of Discovery to the Arctic Ocean*, p. 180. 4to. London, 1835.

but is, if possible, to be avoided, because of the danger of the iceberg overturning or rending asunder, things which occur far more frequently than we should be led to expect from their great appearance of stability. When a ship, notwithstanding every possible caution, is "beset," it is then advisable to "ship" the rudder in order to protect it from injury to which it is peculiarly liable from its unusual weight and size. A ship is exposed to considerable danger when she finds herself among icebergs in a calm; but since these are overspread by a dazzling sheen, even in the thickest mist, the peril of the position is to be avoided at the last moment by warping.

15. As the happy choice of a sea-way is one of the essential conditions of success in ice-navigation, the ability to determine the ship's position and to ascertain whether a surface covered with ice to the horizon, admits of being penetrated, is most desirable. Hence the employment of a balloon would be of the last importance in Arctic navigation. The advantage of being able to ascend from the ship in a balloon secured by a rope, to the height of a few hundred feet is self-evident; and, undoubtedly, the first vessel which avails herself of this great resource will derive extraordinary benefit from it.

16. From the deck of a ship even drift-ice appears

to be of such solidity at a little distance, as to defy navigation, while from the mast-head more water than ice may be descried. In order then to extend the horizon, a look-out, called "the crow's nest," is fixed on the mast-head, in which an officer is always on the watch, and from which all the operations of the vessel are directed. In a ship of the size and height of the *Tegetthoff*, the horizon visible from "the crow's nest" extends to about eleven miles,[1] but at the distance of even five miles the possibility of penetrating cannot be determined with sufficient exactness. It is the business of the officer in the "crow's nest" to observe the passages through the ice and distant objects generally, as he is in the best position to fulfil this most important duty. It is the special business of the watch on the forecastle, to mark what lies in the immediate neighbourhood of the vessel, and his constant care is demanded to avoid isolated ice-floes and prevent collision with them. The seaman at the helm steers the ship by the signs and calls which come to him from the "crow's nest," and modifies them according to those of the watch on the forecastle. The rest of the crew remove the smaller fragments of ice from the vessel's course, special care being taken to prevent their damaging the screw.

[1] When it is not otherwise mentioned, the nautical mile is meant. Four nautical miles make a geographical mile.

17. While sea-currents move the ice in close and continuous lines, winds produce great disturbances in their movement, and open long "leads" in the direction of their course, which often alternate with strips of the thickest pack-ice. This movement of the ice varies with each accumulation of floes, as its rate of motion depends on the height of the ice-field, which then acts as a sail. It is ascertained by experience that calms, on the other hand, have the remarkable property of breaking up the ice. The knowledge and application of these circumstances are essential to the Arctic navigator. If the course of a ship lies across or against a current, it is constantly deflected. The deflection on the coast of East Greenland, for example, amounted to five, even ten miles within twenty-four hours; hence the importance of choosing routes with and not against the course of currents.

18. Lastly, it is of the greatest moment to choose betimes an appropriate winter harbour, and it is therefore necessary to keep near the coast towards the close of the season for navigation. To find one suitable for shelter during the winter in an unknown Arctic region is a matter of great difficulty, for it very often happens, that the ice drifts out from these "docks"[1] in the

[1] *Dock*, an opening in the ice, artificial or natural, offering protection. Kane's *Glossary of Arctic Terms*, vol. i., p. 13.

storms which constantly occur, or perhaps the "dock" is so sheltered, that the ice, if it breaks up at all, breaks up only in the following summer. Shallow bays which freeze almost to the bottom, lying under the Ice of a current or within a fiord, are the most appropriate spots in which to winter.

CHAPTER III.

THE PENETRATION OF THE REGIONS WITHIN THE POLAR CIRCLE; THE PERIOD OF THE NORTH-WEST AND NORTH-EAST PASSAGES.

1. AROUND the lonely apex of the Pole stand cairns of stone which serve to mark the points to which the restless spirit of human enterprise and discovery has penetrated. In its zenith wheels the sea-gull in its flight, and the harpoon-persecuted seal finds on its ice-floes an unapproachable asylum; but the Pole itself remains the goal which no human effort has yet reached.

2. As all knowledge is perfected slowly and gradually, so man's knowledge of the earth and its configuration forms no exception to this general rule. Of the few attempts of early antiquity to enlarge the domain of geographical knowledge, tradition tells us only of the Argonautic expedition of the Greeks, of the voyage of the Phœnicians to Ophir, and their bolder circumnavigation of Africa. With the conception of the spherical form of the earth the still vague notion of

climatal zones makes its appearance, and to this, four centuries before Christ, Pytheas of Marseilles gave the first scientific elucidation and the first approximation to modern theories by his doctrine of the polar circle. Almost contemporaneously Alexander's expedition to the wonder-land of India created a paradise for commerce and navigation, to secure which a shortened route, *the route through the ice*—the most perverse notion that ever entered into the mind of man to conceive—was 1800 years afterwards eagerly and passionately sought.

3. Rome had extended her knowledge to Scandinavia, and Seneca's prophetical mind foresaw the discovery of new worlds. But the deluge of religious strifes, the migrations of nations in the earlier part of the Middle Ages, the holy zeal for destruction in the apostles to the heathen, proved formidable barriers to the extension of geographical knowledge, which were broken through only by the piratical hordes of Normans so renowned in story. While the Romans boasted that Britain had never been circumnavigated, the Normans, throwing the deeds of the Phœnicians into the shade, discovered Greenland, and became *the first Polar Navigators*.

4. Travels by land were the principal means by which the geographical knowledge of the world was enriched; but during the Middle Ages the information which

travellers communicated, uncertain and superficial even for Europe, served only to supply food for the fancies of map-makers, as far as the distant parts of the world were concerned.

5. But the grand moment at length arrived in the history of mankind when the civilization of the West, looking beyond the narrow horizon of the Old World, and awaking from the geographical dreams of centuries, burst the fetters of tradition, and within three hundred years perfected the knowledge of our planet up to the Pole.

6. When by his famous line of partition, Pope Alexander VI. granted to Spain and Portugal the new countries discovered in the East and West, the brigantines of these nations spread themselves over all seas in search of new lands and fresh glory. To the other maritime nations, to the English and the Dutch, nothing remained, if they meant to acquire gold-yielding lands, but to drive the Spaniards and Portuguese from their conquests, or to seek new Eldorados—yea, by the discovery of sea routes on the north of Asia and America, to aspire to India itself. This was the conception first entertained by both the English and the Dutch, and Geography at any rate profited by their delusions. These nations were not to blame if those routes, known afterwards as the *North-West* and *North-*

East passages, degenerated into chimeras, if passages had to be sought in higher and still higher latitudes,—ultimately in the ice itself, although the Dutch geographer, Plancius, struck out the consoling theory of the *open Polar Sea*.

7. But who in those days could presuppose, that the continents of Asia and America, just where those passages were attempted, symmetrically developed the most enormous longitudinal dimensions? Even the actual discovery of the vast extent of Siberia exerted but little influence on the question of the North-East passage, for the achievements of individuals were not then so quickly disseminated as at present. A succession of men in vessels poorly equipped now struggled against the supremacy of the ice, avoiding at first the dreaded wintering, while they attempted sometimes the North-East, sometimes the North-West, sometimes the passage over the Pole itself. In these attempts many lost their lives; many returned, despairing of but still hoping for the solution of the problems —*but no one reached the goal.*

8. The amazing simplicity of the first adventurers is seen in Frobisher's project to erect forts, duly provided with cannons and men, on the commanding points of the passage, in the letters of recommendation given by kings of England to the leaders of the expedition

for the small Saracenic states which were supposed to exist beyond the river Obi; but these old navigators carried no letter of recommendation to the great potentate —the ice. Gold, too, they hoped to find in the North, because the book of Job speaks of gold coming from thence, and the North-East passage was considered as free from danger, because Pliny mentions some Indians who had been driven towards Norway!

9. When another century and a half had elapsed, a series of unsuccessful attempts to force the North-East passage put a decisive check to material interests in Polar expeditions. The North-East passage belonged henceforward to the history of the past. The English and Dutch withdrew from the Novaya Zemlya seas; and after Wood's retreat no scientific expedition entered those seas for two hundred years, *until the days of the Austrian Expeditions.*

10. Among the maritime nations of Europe, it was England, and especially her merchants, who had hitherto largely invested in the costs and risks of these Argonautic expeditions "for the glory of God and the good of the country." The Dutch soon contented themselves, after Barentz's death, with the capture of whales in the Arctic seas; France remained an unconcerned spectator, while the sylphs of Versailles consumed the whalebone of whole fleets of whalers; and Spain and Portugal

early withdrew from seas in which, instead of ingots of gold, ice-floes only were to be found. But even for England the days of the prophets had now passed away—the days of a Cabot, a Mercator,[1] a Wolstenholme, and a Walsingham. Men of weight raised their voices against the chimeras of Arctic commercial routes, and Chillingworth contemptuously compared an expedition for the discovery of the North-East passage to the study of the Fathers.

11. It may be asked, why nations struggled with dauntless ambition for the lost cause of the barren North-West and North-East passages, while for a century they stretched forth timid hands after the rich treasures of lands lying in the more favoured zones? *The mighty stimulus of the love of the marvellous* explains this series of efforts taken up by generation after generation. Frobisher, Davis, Baffin, and the Novaya Zemlya adventurers, told on their return of gold-lands far within the domains of the icy Hydra. Their tales of single combats with spear or matchlock against polar bears, of the dreadful snow-storms and fearful cold of the Arctic winter, were heard with grim delight by listeners on whom no hardships were imposed. Or they spoke of a darkness that continued for months, of the flaming

[1] Mercator was not an Englishman; he was a Dutchman, born 1512, died 1594.

arches of the northern lights, of the sun remaining visible for many weeks in the heavens, of a race of dwarfs, of unheard-of animals, of fish as big as ships of war, of monsters with long teeth which precisely resembled the Sphinxes of the plains of the Pyramids, of white and blue foxes, of floating mountains of dazzling crystal, of ships seen upside down in the air—when had ever the mind of man more food to nourish the love of the marvellous or greater incentives to stimulate the love of distinction? But besides these appeals to the imagination, every generation desires new confirmations of its convictions; and hence geographical questions, after being shelved for a time, come again to the front as by an inward necessity.

12. If the earlier Polar expeditions pursued exclusively material ends, a decided change appears in those of the present century—the Polar world itself became an object of scientific investigation. With Sir John Ross (1818) began a series of expeditions, at first subservient to the idea of a North-West passage, but which ultimately derived all their importance from their attempt—ineffectual as it proved—to rescue the lives of 139 men, who had fallen far from the fields and scenes where earthly fame is commonly achieved. It was these expeditions, still fresh in the memory of this generation, which, summoning to their aid the modern power of

steam against the ice, succeeded in drawing on our Arctic maps a circle whose mean distance was 200 (German) miles from the Pole. Parry on the frozen sea of Spitzbergen had approached it ·within 100 miles (German); Kane, Hayes and Hall on the coast of the Kennedy Channel, the former to within 116; and the two latter to within 108 miles, and the Austro-Hungarian expedition to within 109 miles.

13. MacClintock, who returned with the relics of the Franklin expedition, succeeded in perfecting a mode of discovery independent of the ship—that by means of sledging—admirably adapted for future Arctic expeditions. But the North-West passage for which six generations had toiled, though discovered, was shown to be utterly worthless for all material purposes—a dreary web of coast lines.

CHAPTER IV.

THE INNER POLAR SEA.

1. THE Arctic Sea, in some of its features, forcibly impresses us with its resemblance to the glaciers of the Alps. In both cases, the ice presses from a region, colder and less favoured by climate, towards one warmer and more favoured. In the Alpine glaciers, the movement is from above downwards; in the Frozen Ocean, the movement is from a higher to a lower geographical latitude. In both cases, the tongues and spurs of the masses of ice formed by the configuration of the land or by currents of the sea, terminate, whenever they reach an isothermal curve of altitude or latitude, the mean temperature of which suffices to dissolve them or prevent their formation. Moraines also have their equivalent in the Arctic Sea; for it is an established fact that icebergs and ice-fields, laden with the *débris* and rubbish of Arctic lands, deposit these burdens round the outer edge of the Frozen Ocean, and to this process, partially at least,

the origin of the Newfoundland Banks is ascribed. If this comparison between the phenomena of high latitudes and great altitudes be just, then we should have as much reason to believe in the existence of the so-called open Polar Sea, as we should have to maintain, that in our glacier ranges ice ceases to be formed above a certain altitude.

2. The belief of past times[1] in such a sea shows how unsatisfactory is the simple to man's mind, and how old is his tendency to clothe the remote and the uncommon with a garment of the marvellous. What was the open Polar Sea but the "Harz Sea" of the North, or the legendary zone of the ever-sunny Eden of the Hyperboreans, far beyond the land of the Anthropophagi over which was spread an atmosphere veiled in snow, and through which no light could penetrate! Who has ever seen this open Polar Sea? Do the accounts of navigators confirm its existence? Nay—their accounts are rather a series of counter-statements: Hudson, Baffin, Phipps, Tschitschagoff, Buchan, Franklin, Parry, Collinson, Scoresby, MacClintock, Koldewey, Torell, Nordenskjöld, have all expressed their disbelief in its existence. If some have pretended that they have

---

[1] Three centuries ago, Plancius, the Dutch geographer, devised this for the North Pole, while Barros, the Portuguese historiographer, did the same for the South Pole.

seen it, how strange is it that they never sailed on it! It has recently been attempted to make the great champion of the Polar question, Dr. Petermann, a supporter of this conception; but in the "Mittheilungen" of this highly meritorious geographer, there are many passages which most emphatically protest against it. His views extend only to an inner Polar Sea navigable under certain circumstances, and every one acquainted with those regions may adopt his point of view, though he refuses to admit the existence of the open Polar Sea.

3. In those centuries when the Natural Sciences were little cultivated, when the theories of the Trade Winds, of Equatorial and Polar sea-currents, were still unknown, and when as yet the processes in the Frozen Ocean had not been submitted to scientific investigation, we cannot be surprised at the preconceptions which were formed concerning its phenomena. In those times all beyond Norway was a chaos of ice-filled darkness; the necessity of a scientific investigation of those wastes was not felt; and down to the time of Sir John Ross, Polar navigators on their return home brought with them no kind of scientific knowledge of Nature in the Arctic regions. To reach India was the main if not the only end they had in view. The instructions which Willoughby, the first Polar navigator, received, give us an insight into the delusions of earlier times. These, for example,

warned adventurers against men-eaters who swam naked in the sea, and in the rivers. It was the period of fables long since forgotten. Maldonado, de Fuca, Bernarda, Yelmer, Andrejew, Martinière, and the whale-fishers, brought home tales of passages to India discovered, of new continents, of the ascertained connexion of Novaya Zemlya with the northernmost point of Siberia (Yelmerland) or even with Greenland. Two centuries ago the failure of all attempts at a North-East passage was attributed to Russia's commercial policy inasmuch as it had been proved to the satisfaction of all, that the heat was greater in the north, that the seas there ceased to freeze, and that the country was covered with a luxuriant green!

4. There was, indeed, a certain logical consequence in the belief of an inner Polar Sea, as long as it was unknown that ice is formed on the open sea as well as on the coasts. There was also one argument, which made the existence of such a sea not altogether improbable. It might be assumed, that the formation of ice renewed every year in the Arctic regions, would necessarily produce eternal bulwarks of congelation and destroy all organic life, unless sea-currents modified these extremes of climate. The ice which is formed round the Pole —it was argued—is not of an unlimited but of a definite quantity. Since, then, this quantity of ice must

be brought with tolerable uniformity from the innermost polar region to lower latitudes by the action of sea-currents, there are at least one or two months of the summer when the ice is at a minimum, when no new formation takes place, and when a sea relatively ice-free may appear in the place of the sea which had been covered with ice. This sea would be the more open and navigable, just in proportion as less land might be found at the Pole. But in this assumption it is implied, that the ice moves with perfect regularity and in radial lines from a given point without any disturbance from winds, or counter-currents, or land, consequently with a quiet simplicity of hydrography, for which Nature, neither there nor elsewhere, shows any predilection. Dove makes the mean annual temperature of the North Pole, $-13°·2$ R.; but it is probably still less. What, then, is the probability of an open Polar Sea, if this annual mean only be considered? All the accounts too of animal life increasing in exuberance as we advance northwards—from which a more favourable climate within the innermost Polar region, and an open Polar Sea have been inferred—must be received with caution, for the appearance of numerous flocks of birds proves only, that they remain where open water prevails for a time, and that they change their abode with its change of place.

5. In more recent times great influence has been attributed to the Gulf-stream as a power influencing all the seas, known and unknown, of the whole Arctic region. Dr. Petermann, however, in a lately published work, endeavours to show that its effects are discernible only on the northern seas of Spitzbergen and Novaya Zemlya. Its action on the coasts of Spitzbergen has been indisputably established by the Swedes, who discovered there certain tropical plants (*Entada gigalobium*); but the penetration of the warmer waters of this current to the northern coasts of Novaya Zemlya has not been so positively ascertained. In the Austrian Expedition of 1873-4, we discovered no proofs of its existence. We found neither the constant current, nor the water of a higher temperature, which characterises that renowned stream.

6. For a long time the "ice holes" seen by Wrangel and Morton, were regarded as indications of an ice-free Polar Sea. With regard to those seen by Morton in 81° 22′, Richardson very justly remarks: "The open water of the Kennedy Channel is not of greater extent in the month of June than the open spaces which have occasionally been seen in summer on the north of Spitzbergen by whale-fishers." Wrangel, when he describes the "Polynjii," which he saw on the east of the New Siberian Islands, accounts for them by the action of a

local coast wind; and yet Wrangel would have been the first to favour the notion of an inner Polar Sea, for he still thought, in opposition to Scoresby, that ice could not be formed on the open sea, because of the absence of land as a support for the ice in its formation.

7. The first practical application of the theory of an open Polar Sea was long ago devised by Plancius; the discovery, namely, of a route in high latitudes to China. But the expeditions to the North Pole, properly so termed, sprang also from this theory, which was held with the greatest pertinacity. The evidence of unsuccessful undertakings was always met and outweighed by the counter-experience of one favourable year in the ice. Thus Barentz, in the exceedingly propitious summer of 1594, advanced without difficulty one degree of latitude beyond the northern extremity of Novaya Zemlya, while his successors frequently encountered insurmountable difficulties at Cape Nassau, and he himself in the following year, 1595, found the state of the ice changed much for the worse. In the years 1871, 1874, Mack, Carlsen, and the two Austro-Hungarian expeditions came upon an open sea in the very places where very few, if any, waterways were to be seen in 1872 and 1873. In the summers of 1816, 1817, the mighty stream of ice on the coast of East Greenland had decreased to such an extent that

Scoresby met with little ice between 74° and 80° N.L., but since then whalers have constantly seen the heaviest ice there, heavier than anywhere else. In 1753 and 1754, the Sea of Kara and the Novaya Zemlya Sea were free from ice. But in subsequent years the whale-fishers knocked in vain at their ice-barred entrances. In 1823 Lütke from a point on the west coast of the Sea of Kara saw that sea without ice; but, in the middle of August, 1833, Pachtussow found the western side of that sea open, while in the previous year he himself could not pass the Karian Gates. Again in 1743 and 1773, the North Spitzbergen Sea held out promises the most inviting, which might possibly have permitted the reaching of a still higher degree of latitude than that which Nordenskjöld and Koldewey attained in 1868. Sir John Ross, in the first year of his second voyage, found all things most favourable for navigation, but in the following year the very reverse; and Sir James C. Ross experienced the same alternation of circumstances in the Southern Polar Sea. In 1850, Penny found the Wellington Channel free from ice, but in 1852, Belcher, although he penetrated far further than Penny, was confronted in the same channel by pack and drift-ice. Scoresby the younger, to whose profound faculty of observation we owe the most significant hints on the nature of the Polar Sea, although he had navigated the Greenland ice-ocean for twenty years, landed only once on its coast. The Swedish expedition (1861) could approach the north-east of Spitzbergen only in boats; Smith sailed over the sea there (1871) as far as Cape Smith. The walrus hunter, Matilas, sailed round (1864) the north-east island completely, and Carlsen, an ice navigator, as successful as he was skilful, in 1863 circumnavigated Spitzbergen, and in 1871, Novaya Zemlya, and discovered there the relics of Barentz's winter quarters. In 1872, King Karl Land was circumnavigated, although both Koldewey and Nordenskjöld (1868) as well as the first Austrian expedition (1871) had in vain attempted to approach it. How greatly also, in the same year, the state of the ice varies in different places, is proved by the fact, that Franklin learnt from the whalers that they never saw the ice so thick and so strong in Davis Straits as at the end of July, 1819, while Parry, more to the north by some degrees of latitude, pursued his path of discovery even to Melville Island, and in the following year returned to England without meeting any special obstacles. These examples, to which many more might be added, show how variable are the chances of ice-navigation from one year to another. But however variable the conditions of the ice may be, the impediments, even under the most favourable circumstances, are so very great, that we have never been able to penetrate the innermost polar regions, —*penetrate*, that is, *to where, according to the views of an earlier time, the open Polar Sea should be found.*

8. Those propitious ice-years amount, therefore, to nothing more than a greater recession of the outer ice-barrier—trifling when compared with the mighty whole —or to an increased navigability of certain coast waters, or to a local loosening of the inner polar ice-net. In reality the whole Arctic Sea, with its countless ice-fields and floes, and its web of fine interlacing water-ways, is nothing but a net constantly in motion from local, terrestrial, or cosmical causes. All the changes and phenomena of this mighty network lead us to infer the existence of frozen seas up to the Pole itself; and according to my own experience gained in three expeditions I consider *that the states of the ice between* $82°$ *and* $90°$ *N.L. will not essentially differ from those which have been observed south of latitude* $82°$; *I incline rather to the belief that they will be found worse instead of better.*

9. If this view be correct, it will remain an insuperable difficulty to reach the Pole with a ship. The penetrating to $82°$ or $83°$ exhausts, according to all past experience, the disposable time for navigation, and presupposes moreover the most favourable conditions for the attaining of such high latitudes. A ship which

E 2

reaches 82° N.L. by the beginning of autumn must risk nothing more, should only navigate really open water, and the expediency of securing a winter harbour should then outweigh every other consideration.

10. He who expects with a ship of the present construction to reach the Pole in a single summer, necessarily believes in an ocean at the Pole. But even if an expedition should penetrate to 84° in Smith's Sound, or should reach Cape Tcheljuskin on the north-east route, it would not follow that such an ocean exists, but only that the Polar Sea presents at different times and in different places open water-ways, which may enable a ship to advance beyond a point hitherto reached; but it is improbable that the circumstances which favoured this will be repeated the next summer, so as to permit the ships to penetrate still further—or to return. The last American expedition returned without being able to speak decisively as to the possibility of navigating Lincoln Sea, and since this has not yet been verified by fact, we must suspend our judgment on the matter. To the English expedition, which has taken this route to the Pole, is reserved the great work of throwing light on the region of Upper Smith's Sound, and the whole civilized world will hail with joy any successes which a nation, so long conspicuous for its perseverance in the cause of discovery, may happily achieve.

CHAPTER V.

THE FUTURE OF THE POLAR QUESTION.

1. THE eagerness of human nature for gain and material prosperity is so great, that we are wont to estimate the value of all undertakings by the standard of utility; and too often it is forgotten, that each generation is destined to fulfil the task of acquiring and collecting the knowledge which is to benefit only a later generation. If, then, the Polar question be valueless for our material interests, is it therefore valueless for science? and assuming that it is for the present worthless as far as gain and wealth are concerned, must it continue so for all time? Not that we are entitled, even from this narrower point of view, to deny the usefulness of Polar exploration, as Cook seems to have done when he said, "Never from those regions will any advantage accrue to our race;" but rather bear in mind what Sir James Ross tells us: "The profit which accrued to England, in each year after the voyage (1818) of my

uncle (Sir John Ross) in North Baffin's Bay, from those rediscovered parts of the Arctic seas, was more than enough to defray all the expenses of the voyages of discovery undertaken from 1818 to 1838." Scoresby with his single ship made a million thalers by the capture of whales, and the Americans had for many years a clear profit of eight million dollars from the fisheries of the frozen seas of Behring's Straits. There were also, it is true, very considerable losses; for, in 1830, nineteen English ships engaged in the whale fishery were "beset" in the ice of Melville Bay, and nearly all destroyed; in 1871, twenty-six American ships were crushed to pieces in Behring's Straits, and as many as seventy-three Dutch vessels sank in one year in the seventeenth century from the pressure of the ice.

2. We do not, however, mean to assert, that the progress of Polar discovery is always followed by a corresponding increase in the capture of fish in the Arctic seas. On the contrary, the take of oil-yielding animals is steadily decreasing, and even if an open sea should be discovered in 82° N.L., in which whales should be found in as great abundance as ice-floes unhappily are, the whaler with his poor equipment would never be able to follow them thither. The fur countries, once as productive as the mines of Peru, are incapable of further extension; even the treasures of mammoth's tusks have

become rare, and in order to bring thirty tons of lignite from the north-east of Greenland, a ship must expend seventy tons of sound coal in the transit, besides passing the winter there. That the teas of China, the silks of Japan, the spices of the Moluccas will never descend to us from the ice-fields, has long been settled. No one at the present day thinks any longer of the commercial value of the North-West and North-East passages. Modes of escape from the perils and caprices of the ice have grown out of the endeavour to discover routes of commerce, which lay beyond the reach of the cannon of the Spaniards at the time when they aspired to the monopoly of the trade of the world. The reward of 25,000 gulden, offered by the Dutch government for the discovery of a North-East passage, and that of £20,000 by the English parliament for the North-West passage, have never been paid, because never claimed, nor are they, in the least degree, likely to be claimed.[1]

3. Yet, quite independent of material results, Polar exploration presents no unworthy object for scientific investigation—a region of the globe 120,000 square miles in extent never yet entered by man. The Polar question, as *a problem of science*, aims at determining the

---

[1] As a corrective to this rather extreme statement, see Clement Markham's *Threshold of the Unknown Region*, 4th Edition, pp. 383—393.

limits of land and water, at the perfecting of that network of lines with which comparative science seeks to surround our planet, even to its Poles. The completion of this labour will serve to discover those physical laws which regulate climates, the currents of the atmosphere and sea, and the analogies of geology with the earth as we see it.

4. But how is this to be attained? At first it would appear as if the methods of ice-navigation had been followed by such success, that their continued application guaranteed still greater results. The gradual advance by means of ships, from the Polar Circle to 73°, 75°, 79°, or even to 82° N.L., has been the result and is the reward of the labours of three centuries. But to reach higher degrees, from 82° to 90°, depends on other conditions than mere time. That increased experience and boldness have removed many of the inconveniences and dangers attendant on Arctic navigation is undoubtedly true, but it is also as true, that, upon the whole, *the safety and convenience of ice-navigation have more steadily increased than its successes.* Hudson, Baffin, and especially Scoresby, and even some whalers of the seventeenth century, reached latitudes which have scarcely been exceeded since, and in many cases this progress was due, not to greater boldness and experience, but rather to chance and

the caprices of the ice, which "to the whaler often permitted glances into its interior, which were denied to the scientific explorer."

5. The greater perfection of our means enables us to conduct Polar expeditions with greater facility. Instead of dissipating our strength by sending out several ships, even small fleets, amounting sometimes to fifteen ships (often not larger than the boats of a modern Polar ship), since the days of Sir John Ross, we equip one or two ships only, strongly built for their special purpose, provided with steam-power, and with all that is desirable or requisite; and instead of dispatching them for short summer cruises, we provision them, send them out for several years, and, by appropriate nourishment and the aid of medical science, protect the crews from the scourge of scurvy. In those days, when even the wealthy lived during the winter on salt beef, and English squires were obliged at the beginning of winter, on account of the scarcity of food for the cattle, to kill and salt a portion of their herd, preserved and antiscorbutic victuals were an impossibility to a Hudson, a James, a Fox, in their winters amid the ice. Those introduced by Ross—then called "Donkin's meat"—have been greatly improved since, and through them the scurvy, which used to carry off whole crews of ships, has lost its former terrors.

6. In this power to extend our expeditions without danger, and especially in sledge journeys during the autumn and spring, which are possible only to expeditions prepared to winter in the ice, are the grounds why we have not halted at the barriers "of the bulwarks built for eternity;" in the Rennselaer harbour, in the Lancaster-Barrow route, or at the Pendulum islands. It is only sledge expeditions, as Middendorf says, which have been able to effect results of any magnitude on the inaccessible coasts of the extreme north; and the great extent to which the Russians had used sledge expeditions evidently served as an example both to the English and to Kane.

7. In Polar expeditions, therefore, we have probably reached, so far as the exploration of the highest latitudes by means of ships is concerned, the limits of possibility. The extraordinary success which fell to the lot of Hall's expedition *teaches us only the possibility of encroaching but a little beyond that limit,* even under the most favourable circumstances.

8. In all cases, where the attempt shall be made to reach the highest latitudes with a ship, I would again recommend the route through Smith's Sound, because, in the first place, I believe that any considerable advance is only to be expected in coast-water; and in the second place, because the Grant Coast offers facilities for

sledge expeditions on a large scale. East Greenland in the higher latitudes, 73°—75°, may be regarded as inaccessible; and the attempt to penetrate northwards in its coast-water was a delusion of the second German North-Pole Expedition. In the north of Spitzbergen, and in Behring's Straits, fifty expeditions and countless whalers have heard from the ice an imperious *ne plus ultra*; and the same prohibition has been uttered to as many expeditions on the North-East passage. In both these routes the cause of failure was the disproportion between what could be reached in one or two summers, and the vast extent of sea blocked by impenetrable ice. In like manner, the probability of reaching the Pole itself with our present resources is so small, and the attempt to do it is so utterly disproportionate to the sacrifices exacted and the results achieved, that it would be advisable to exclude it from Arctic exploration, until, instead of the impotent vessels of the sea, we can send thither those of the air.

9. Be this as it may, the present English North Pole Expedition will essentially contribute to solve the question, whether the Pole can be reached by the route through Upper Smith's Sound. This, according to the views of almost all Polar navigators, holds out the greatest chances for further advance by sea. Should this expedition, equipped in so effective a manner, and

sent out by a nation of such great experience, not come nearer to the goal, or, if nearer, only through sledging—which may very probably be the case—the conviction will then be strengthened, that all efforts to reach the Pole by navigation in the Frozen Ocean are hopeless, and witness only to the glorious persistency of human endeavour.

10. But until aërial navigation to the Pole shall be attempted, it would be advisable to follow the example of the Swedes, and, in the service of Natural History and Geography, content ourselves with the exploration of those Arctic lands of which, up to the present moment, we know only the coast-line, or which, situated on the outermost verge of our Polar charts, are still untrodden by man; we mean specially Gillis', Grinnell's, Wrangel's Land, and above all, the interior of Greenland. The Polar question, hitherto regarded chiefly as a geographical problem, would thus, for a considerable time, be taken up in the interests of Natural Science. Lieutenant Weyprecht, after dwelling on the predominance of exploration in Polar expeditions, expresses a wish, that the great civilized nations would unite in contemporaneous Arctic expeditions for magnetical, electrical, and meteorological investigations: "In order to attain decisive scientific results, a number of expeditions should be sent to different places in the Arctic regions

to make observations, at the same time, with similar instruments, and in accordance with similar instructions." They who think such results too insignificant for the energies and sacrifices which are expended to achieve them, and who would rather that such efforts should be transferred to those still unknown regions of the earth, which may become the dwelling-places of man, will, of course, give their veto against the further agitation of the Arctic question.

CHAPTER VI.

POLAR EQUIPMENTS.

1. EVERY Arctic expedition should be guided by the experience of its predecessors, both in its plan and its equipment; and hence we have often to deplore the negligence of almost all polar navigators in failing to inform those who follow them of what they actually saw, of their modes of procedure, or of the mistakes which they committed. It will not, therefore, be labour thrown away, if we state our own experience and record our own observations for the guidance of others, in order to show, with the utmost possible clearness, what future explorers have before them, and how best to meet it.

2. Undivided command in an expedition is the first of all rules; but if there be any division of command in a subordinate expedition by sea or land, the duties and rights of its commander must be clearly and exactly defined. In recent times the command of a

Polar expedition has sometimes been conferred not on a seaman, but on a man of science, as in the cases of Kane, Hayes, Nordenskjöld, and Torell. Where the investigation of questions connected with Natural History is the aim and object, this precedent is admissible, but it should never be observed, where the commander has an important part to fulfil as a navigator. The command of an expedition has never been conferred on a man of science by the English government. In the very commencement, indeed, of Polar discovery, an English expedition was placed under the command of Sir Hugh Willoughby, who was not bred a sailor, but down to the seventeenth century even in their naval campaigns, such men were appointed to naval commands. The Dutch expeditions of the sixteenth century generally adopted a destructive division of command, under supercargoes and pilots, representing the mercantile and nautical elements: confusion and discord were the inevitable consequences.

3. Next to the selection of a commander, the selection of the crew demands the greatest care. This ought to be made some time before the expedition starts, in order that those unfit for the service may be discovered, and their places supplied by others; this cautious mode of procedure, and not a preference for any particular nationality, will secure the most effective

crew. Although seamanlike qualities do not belong in the same degree to every nation, time and pains only are needed to secure a picked crew for a North Pole expedition from almost any nation. Endurance of cold is not the only test of effectiveness, although this is a very common assumption; but a sense of duty, perseverance, and resolution are the virtues of a seaman. Habit soon teaches men to conquer cold, and inexorable necessity often hardens weaklings into heroes for Arctic discovery. A certain degree of intelligence is of high importance in the crew. In many cases resolution in the midst of dangers depends on their capacity to observe and think, even on their possessing certain branches of knowledge. The greater part of the crew of the *Tegetthoff* had these advantages. But men who, in a heavily-laden sledge, leave the old and take to recently-formed ice, without noticing the difference,—who observe a frost-bitten foot several hours after the mischief has been done,—who lose their cartridges, know nothing of their rifle, and little more of their compass, or who pass on without observing the configurations of the land, possess an indifference indeed, but of a kind very dangerous to themselves and to the whole party, though they may despise death as much as Achilles is said to have done.

4. An intelligent crew, from their greater feeling

of independence, is, however, more difficult to command than an ignorant one. Devotion and blind confidence are more rarely found in an educated crew; their amenability to discipline is dependent on the good example, the kindness, and unalterable calmness of those who may command them. The law of a Polar expedition is obedience, and its basis morality. Punishments are in such situations a miserable and depressing means for the preservation of order, and their employment, especially in a private undertaking, will tend rather to loosen than to maintain the bonds of discipline. If Parry, in 1820, caused corporal punishment to be inflicted, this proves the greater facility with which discipline is maintained on board of a man-of-war, but not its appropriateness generally. Coercion and threats produce no effect; and hence the folly of attempting to secure success by sending out again those who returned without having achieved anything, which was done last century by the authorities at St. Petersburg with every unsuccessful enterprise on the Arctic coasts of Siberia. The regulation that the most meritorious among the crew shall be specially rewarded, after the return of the expedition, provides for the recognition of merit, without exciting ill feeling in the less worthy. For the officers scientific success may be a perfect reward of their toils, but for the crew the reward should consist of more material advantages. Money, indeed, seems a feeble motive of action to men destined to withstand for years the inclemency of Arctic winters, and uncertain whether they shall ever return; but, notwithstanding, it is the only form by which men without sympathy for the aims of science can be gained for the attainment of such objects. The crews of Sir John Ross received for a martyrdom of four years passed in the ice about £100 a head; in the second German expedition from eight to twelve thalers were the monthly pay of each sailor. The pay of the sledgers in the *Tegetthoff* was, however, nearly four times as much; in some sledge journeys it amounted to 3,000 gulden a man.

5. Contrary to what might be expected, the re-employment of those who have served before, is not to be recommended as a rule. The very best only should be re-enlisted. The others are too much disposed to place their experience on a level with that of their commanders; and in all cases, where their opinions differ from those of their officers, they damage by a kind of passive opposition the fundamental law of an expedition—obedience. Those who enter the Arctic regions for the first time are wont to receive the orders of an experienced commander with an attention as unquestioning as it is respectful. Married men also should be

excluded, as they were by Barentz in his second (1596) expedition.

6. Some of the crew should be good shots, good pedestrians and mountaineers, but all must be of the same nationality, and in perfect health. The least symptom of rheumatism, of diseases of the lungs and the eyes, and of certain chronic maladies only too common among seamen, unfit them for the endurance of the Polar climate, and especially for sledge expeditions. Those who are addicted to drink are peculiarly liable to the scurvy.

7. The medical man of an expedition, besides professional skill and experience, must possess the most imperturbable patience, for to many of his patients he is not less a physician of the mind than of the body. He should convince himself of the sanitary condition of the crew before the expedition starts, although it may have been previously investigated by medical authorities and declared satisfactory.

8. Since an expedition, in addition to its scientific functions, should take up the illustration of Nature at the Pole, the employment of a photographer, but still better of an artist, is very desirable, for the former is too much confined to the immediate neighbourhood of the ship in his operations.

9. The records of Arctic adventure in former days

tell us of equipments strangely incompatible with the object pursued. Their commercial purpose constrained them to fill the hold with bales of silk, instead of provisions for years; but the letters of recommendation which were given to the explorers of the North-East passage for the Saracen princes on the route to Chatai seem peculiarly ludicrous. Some justification may be discovered for Owczyn taking a priest with him on his Siberian expedition (1734), but hardly for his wanting fifty-seven men in a vessel only seventy feet long, and arming it with eight falconets. The employment of a drummer, twelve privates and a corporal, on Gmelin's scientific Siberian expedition, is still more unintelligible; more so than Davis's band of music, which was intended to charm the feelings of the Eskimos and dispose them to peaceful proceedings, his predecessor Frobisher having had the saddest experience of their barbarism. Other expeditions by the too plentiful distribution of knives and hatchets among the Eskimos placed them in a position seriously to threaten the white man, and even at the present day the so-called "Wilden-kiste" often contains articles little calculated to inspire the natives with a high opinion of our moral superiority.

10. In fitting out a Polar expedition, all respect should be paid to the principle of bestowing on those who are for a time banished, the greatest possible amount of comfort.

The proportions of a ship, and the space at its disposal, narrow the limits available for this end; and since the return to the employment, as at the first, of small vessels, even these limits have been considerably diminished.

11. The following table shows that the employment of small vessels was the principle at first followed, although the English undertakings even of this present century never thoroughly adopted the example of a Fotherby, a Baffin, and a Ross:—

The Expeditions of	A.D.	Tonnage of the Ships.			Provisioned for	Crew.
Willoughby . .	1553	120	90	160	18 months	...
Frobisher . .	1576	25	25	10	⎫	...
„ . .	1577	180	30	30	⎬	...
Pett Jackman .	1580	40	20	...	⎭	15
Davis	1585	50	35	...		42
„	2nd expedn.	10	50	53 120		...
Weymouth . .	1604	70	60	...		...
Knight . . .	1606	40	...	...	Mostly for ⎫	...
Hudson . . .	1607	...	...	...	one year ⎬	10
„ . . .	1608	...	...	...	only. ⎭	15
James Poole . .	1609	70	...	...	....	15
Hudson . . .	1610	55	...	...		...
Smith	1610	50	...	...		...
James Poole. .	1611	50	...	...		...
Fotherby . . .	1615	20	...	...		...
Baffin	1616	58	...	...		...
Fox	1631	80	...	...	18 months	20
James	1631	70	...	...	18 „	...
Wood	1676	...	...	...	16 „	19
Moor . . .	1746	180	140	...	...	...
Ross	1818	385	252	...	...	...
Parry	1819	375	180	...	2½ years	...
Lütke	1821	200	...	...	...	45
Hayes	1860	133	...	...	1½ „	15
Koldewey . .	1869	180	200	...	2 „	20

12. The inspection of this table shows that it was the practice of the sixteenth century to send out fleets of ships of a very small size, that in the seventeenth one small ship was commissioned, and that the employment of two vessels has been the rule since; and this would have been still more evident, if the various Franklin expeditions had been included in the above table. In 1829 Sir John Ross started with a ship drawing eighteen feet, but changed afterwards to one drawing eight feet; and from eight to twelve feet is now the recognised draught in Polar-ships. Large vessels require a numerous crew, and if they have not been built exclusively for the purpose of Polar exploration, their small economy of space prevents their being fitted out for more than two years and a half. In 1819 Parry's ship, the large *Fury*, had, with a draught of eighteen feet, provisions for only two and a half years, whereas the *Victory* (1829) of Ross with only seven feet draught had on board, besides stores for the same period, a steam-engine and coals for a thousand hours' steaming. The Russian Novaya-Zemlya navigators of this century have adopted vessels of a size which must be destructive of all comfort and convenience. These vessels are thirty or forty feet long, with a draught of five or six feet, and a crew of nine or ten men. But Arctic ships must have a crew above the ordinary strength and be

provided with steam-power; so that, allowing for the necessary space for the quarters of the crew, for the engines and the coalbunkers, little room will be left for the stowage of stores. But this little should be reserved for well-chosen provisions stowed away so as to avoid all empty spaces, and secure the greatest amount of resistance to lateral pressure. The weakest parts of a ship are always the spaces left for air in the quarters of the men. A crew, which is exposed to threatening dangers from the ice, will never regret the strengthening of these void spaces by heavy horizontal tie-beams, removable when the ship is in the winter harbour, and so adjusted as not to impede communication. The mere suspension of heavy beams against the hull of a ship does not always answer the purpose of protection, since the pressure of the ice frequently drives away these protecting timbers. The practice, however, is not absolutely to be rejected.

13. The daily allowance of solid food for the effectives in an Arctic expedition amounts to about two pounds, and in sledge expeditions to $2\frac{3}{4}$ pounds, of which half a pound is bread and one pound preserved meat. Besides the usual provisions, large supplies of preserved vegetables, of cocoa, of extract of meat, of rice, of preserved peas, of dried farinaceous food (such as macaroni), are very desirable. Salted

meat is to be avoided as much as possible. The luxury of fresh bread twice a week instead of the hard ship's biscuit is an essential means of promoting health, and the want of yeast for its preparation may be supplied by "baking powder." Once a day a ration of lemon-juice should be served out as a preservative against scurvy, and anti-scorbutic victuals should be laid in abundantly. Plenty of tea and tobacco is indispensable; the want of these is painfully felt, especially by the sailors. Cases have actually occurred, where crews have ground the wooden blocks of the rigging to powder, to serve as tea, and have used the hoops of casks for tobacco.

14. The moderate enjoyment of spirituous liquors is much to be recommended, as their influence on health and sociality is of great importance. The preservation, however, of a sufficient stock of wine especially in winter is a matter of much difficulty, since most kinds freeze at $-5°$ or $-8°$ R. As long as the ship is afloat, as it generally is when winters are passed in the ice, it is advisable to preserve the supply of wine at the bottom of the hold and to place all other things most liable to be frozen in layers above it. But if a ship be nearly or entirely out of water, it is advisable to keep the wine, and other indispensable liquids, in the empty spaces of the cabin, under the cabin table, near the stove, below the berths and under the sky-light after it

has been closed for the winter. Only absolute want of space justifies the preparation of *chemical wine*,[1] since the volume of its constituent parts without water is only a fifth of real wine; and under all circumstances *chemical wine* is but a miserable shift, and the beer (even the spruce beer of Sir John Ross) which the English used to manufacture on board ship from the essence of malt and hops is far preferable. The rum and cognac, especially for sledge expeditions, in order to save weight should contain the greatest possible amount of alcohol, for its dilution before use is a matter of no difficulty.

15. During the winter, residence in the ship itself is preferable to living in log-houses, because the ship can be more easily heated and suffers less from the accumulation of ice. But since a ship in the Arctic Sea ceases for ten months of the year to be a ship and becomes in fact a house, this should be kept in view when she is being fitted out.

16. The place where the men live is always in the fore-part of the ship, but their berths should be changed in a certain rotation, because of the inequality of the condensation. It is not advisable to place the kitchen in the quarters of the crew in order to diminish the

---

[1] A decoction prepared by Dr. Kepes, the physician of the *Tegetthoff*.

consumption of coals, because an accumulation of moisture is thereby increased. The officers and *savans* occupy a common mess-room in the after part of the ship, and sleep in little cabins ranged round it. The power to withdraw occasionally from the presence of those who must be together for years is an important element of harmony. Sir John Ross and his officers in 1833, even in the miserable hut built on the Fury coast, did not occupy the common messroom heated by a stove, but preferred separate cabins, the temperature of which seldom rose above the freezing point, and in which they had to suffer much from the accumulation of ice. All the living rooms should be provided with waterproof carpets. Their heating by means of the common stoves is objectionable, because of the unequal distribution of warmth. An even temperature is best maintained by the use of the Meidinger "Fullofen," which has the further advantage of consuming only a small quantity of coals. Hot-air flues are, perhaps, preferable even to these, because they better prevent the freezing of the moisture in the cabins, and indeed in every part of the ship.

17. An Arctic ship should be provided with an iron-plated washing and drying closet, without which the washing of linen would be restricted to the few weeks of summer weather. This closet may also be used as

a bath room, an important means of promoting health. The lighting of the living rooms by petroleum sufficiently answers all purposes; in the cabins, however, stearine candles are to be preferred either to it or any other oil. The construction of the lamps used in making observations in the open air during the long Arctic darkness is a matter of the greatest importance. Those used in the second German North-Pole expedition were of peculiar excellence, and never failed in their difficult service. Massive lamps, with glass globes protected with wire, and burning petroleum in preference to common oil, should be used on deck, and as they are employed for so many purposes and exposed to so many risks, a plentiful supply of them should be provided. In the huts on the deck, built over the hatchways, train-oil may be used with advantage, if the lamps are so constructed that the flame may heat the reservoir containing the oil.

18. So long as the crew remains on board the ship, their clothing, even in the severest winter, needs but little attention. Thick close-fitting woollen under garments, knitted woollen gloves, outer garments of strong cloth, are in all cases sufficient on deck, and in all those parts of the ship which are kept at a certain temperature. Leather boots lined with fur were long considered an indispensable requisite for Polar expeditions, but they

have not maintained their character, as they are very heavy, become unpliable in frost, and soon quite useless through its action and the wearing off of the fur.

19. Before the departure of the expedition, all the instruments should be thoroughly cleansed from oil by a practical optician, and the firearms should undergo a like operation at the hands of the gunmaker, and their barrels should be browned to protect them better from rust. The ammunition, powder and matches to blast the ice, alcohol and petroleum, should be stowed in the after-part of the ship, and the two latter should be reached only through a closely-fitting pump. A very ample supply of alcohol, flannel, buffalo-skins, strong cloth, water-proof canvas, felt, leather, rein-deer shoes, snow boots, shovels, cramp irons, poles, &c. ; articles, which are too often overlooked, should be taken both from their usefulness on board ship, and also on land expeditions.

20. The costs of Polar expeditions have relatively rather diminished than increased. The expenses of Willoughby's expedition 300 years ago amounted to the sum—quite enormous for that day—of £6,000 ; Moor's (1746) cost £10,000 ; while Back's difficult but successful undertaking to explore the great Fish-river (1833—1835), only £5,000. The Siberian expedition of Middendorf (1844)—costing only 13,300

rubles (£1,717)—was a matchless example of extraordinary achievements with little expenditure. The costs of the various Franklin expeditions from 1848 to 1854 amounted, according to the statement of the English Admiralty, to twenty million francs (£833,333): those of the second German North-Pole expedition to 120,000 thalers (£11,000), and the expenses of our own Austrian-Hungarian North-pole expedition to 220,000 gulden (£18,333.)

THE PIONEER VOYAGE OF
THE ISBJÖRN.

JUNE 20—OCTOBER 4, 1871.

THE PIONEER VOYAGE OF THE "ISBJÖRN."

1. THE failure of the second German Arctic expedition directed the future efforts of Polar exploration to the seas of Novaya Zemlya. Although the geographical position and political relations of Austria prevented its Government from taking any active part in the great geographical problems and questions of our times, an interest in Polar discovery had been excited in her statesmen, which gradually ripened into a determination to send its flag, renowned for its military fame, to consecrate struggles on the peaceful domain of scientific exploration. The magnanimous act of Graf Wilczek, contributing 40,000 florins towards the equipment of an Austro-Hungarian expedition, not only strengthened but also endowed the resolve. In order, however, to obviate the possibility of spending large sums on a plan which might be unfeasible, or if feasible, of little value, it was determined to despatch a pioneer expedition to the

seas of Novaya Zemlya under the joint command of Lieutenant Weyprecht and myself. The knowledge and experience gained in that voyage—which is described in the following pages—induced the Austrian Government to send another and more powerful vessel to those seas, equipped to pass two or more winters in the ice.

2. It seemed to be established as the result of many expeditions, that almost invincible difficulties opposed the reaching of the central Arctic regions by the routes through Baffin's Bay, Behring's Straits, along the coast of Greenland, and from Spitzbergen, mainly because on them all we are met by the great Arctic currents, which act as channels to carry off the ice of the Polar basin. These currents carry with them vast masses of ice, which they deposit on all the coasts which they strike. On the results of many Norwegian, Russian, and German voyages, partly in the interests of science, partly in the interests of commerce, many geographers maintained that the traces of the Gulf Stream did not disappear at the North Cape, but rather that it exercised a considerable influence on places and in latitudes not before imagined, as, for instance, on the North-east coasts of Novaya Zemlya. An expedition, therefore, which followed the course of the warmer waters of the Gulf Stream would find fewer and less

formidable obstacles, than on the routes exposed to the Arctic currents, carrying with them colossal masses of ice towards the south. On the east of Spitzbergen there is a land which has, indeed, been often seen, but never reached, or even attempted to be reached—Gillis' Land —lying in the course of the Gulf Stream ; and it is a probable assumption, that navigable water would be found under its western coast, as at Spitzbergen, where 80° N. Lat. can be reached every year without any difficulty. If, then, this stream extends still further to the north—which is probable according to the soundings taken by the Swedes—it is reasonable to expect, that higher latitudes may be reached on this than on any other route.

3. It is remarkable, that the seas between Spitzbergen and Novaya Zemlya were utterly unknown to science. No expedition had ever been sent thither, though many things seemed to invite and favour the venture, and Dr. Petermann had long endeavoured to organize a powerful and well-equipped expedition to explore higher latitudes on this route. At length Lieutenant Weyprecht and I undertook a voyage of reconnaissance to those waters, in order to ascertain whether the climate and the state of the ice were as favourable in reality, as they seemed to be in theory. No attempt was to be made to reach high latitudes or to make

important geographical discoveries. The small means at our command forbade either. Our aims were more limited; they referred to the temperature of the water and the air, to the currents, to the state of the ice, to the probability of success in the following year (1872), and lastly, to opportunities for extended sledge journeys. We were to sail from Tromsoe about the middle of June, and return thither by the middle of September.

4. In order to diminish expenses, we chartered at Tromsoe a small sailing ship. A steamer would, indeed, have been more serviceable, but the cost would have been quadrupled, without any adequate advantage. The *Isbjörn* (i.e., Ice-bear) was a vessel of fifty tons, cutter-rigged, 55 feet long, 17 feet broad, with a draught of 6 feet. Her bows were protected with sheet-iron, two feet above, and two feet under, water. She was new and strong, and made with us her first voyage. We had also two small boats, and a so-called "Fang-boot"— whale-boat. She was commanded by Captain Kjelsen, and had as a crew a harpooner, four sailors, a carpenter, and a cook—all Norwegians. We were provided with the requisite instruments by the Imperial · Geographical Institute, and were provisioned for four or five months. The Austrian Consul Aagaard aided us to

the utmost of his ability in the equipment of the vessel. It must be observed, that we had no direct command or control over the vessel and its crew; the responsibility for the ship, and the immediate command over its crew, belonged to the skipper Kjelsen. Weyprecht was however, the real commander.

5. The information we gathered concerning the state of the ice in the region of our projected exploration, was exceedingly contradictory. While, for example, Dr. Bessels, in the steamer *Albert*, of Rosendal, discovered a branch of the Gulf Stream with a temperature of $+4°$ R. at the ice-barrier on the south of Gillis' Land, Dr. Petermann sent us a letter of Lamont, in which he said: "Every year the ice appears to me more formidable." The whalers of Tromsoe, who knew the ice of that region only from hearsay, and could give no positive information as to its limits, uttered many unfavourable prognostications as to the possibility of penetrating that frozen sea, or of approaching Gillis' Land from the south. The region was utterly unknown, even to many skippers who sailed from Spitzbergen to Novaya Zemlya. The few attempts to penetrate to that land, first seen in 1707, and regarded by the Swedes as a continent, had been unsuccessful. So also their efforts to reach it from the South-west

in 1864 and 1868. Captain Koldewey's attempt also, which was made from the "Thousand Isles" three months before the last-named voyage, had been attended with the same want of success. None of these expeditions had passed beyond the ice-barrier, and their failures contributed greatly to strengthen the opinion, that the Novaya Zemlya seas were unnavigable.

6. All our inquiries were met also with the prediction of an exceedingly unfavourable year for the ice. The spring of 1871 had been unusually severe, and even to the middle of June the northern parts of Norway were covered with a mantle of snow reaching down to the sea. It was inferred, therefore, that there would be an excessive accumulation of ice in the seas further north. We heard even, that there was ice at the distance of about twenty (Norwegian) miles from North Cape. And it was certainly true, that the north winds, which prevailed for some weeks, kept a number of Norwegian fishing and seal-hunting vessels weatherbound off the "Scheeren." All this notwithstanding, we determined to keep to our plan of sailing to Hope Island, and of following from thence the ice-barrier towards the east, our progress, of course, being dependent on favourable conditions of the ice, and perhaps on the influences of the Gulf Stream. As it was within the verge of possibility to make Gillis' Land

during the season of our operations, we considered it advisable not to pass beyond 40° E. Long. while we penetrated northward.

7. On the 20th of June we left Tromsoe during a drizzling snow-storm, and while we were sailing up the "Qualsund" without a pilot, we touched the ground—a danger we incurred from the desire of our married sailors to put their wives ashore, after leave-taking, as near the land as possible. At Rysoe we fell in with the fleet of the Tromsoe fishing-boats at anchor, waiting for a change of weather, and with them some vessels which, we thought, would have been by this time in the ice, having left Tromsoe four weeks before.

8. The rocky islands off the coast of Finnmark are surrounded by bleak cliffs, rising to the height of 2,500 feet, and upwards. Trees cease to grow there; occasionally the birch appears, but never in sufficient numbers to form a wood. The numerous islands of a gneiss formation show the same landscape which characterizes Norway—indescribably bleak table-lands, deep secluded valleys and gorges, interspersed with lonely mountain lakes. The bold, picturesque outlines of these islands are exceedingly striking, though their fertility is meagre in the extreme. The solitary rocky shores are inhabited by poor families, secluded from the

world, and having little intercourse with each other. They live for the most part on the fish which they catch. The remains of fish round these settlements render their approach exceedingly disagreeable; on the Lofodden Islands a guano manufactory has been established, which turns this refuse to good account. Tromsoe or Hammerfest appear in their eyes as the glory and pride of the world. We were detained two days—June 24 and 25—by contrary winds, at Sandoe, an island covered with sea-sand full of small mussel shells, to the height of 600 feet. Ascending an elevated peak of this island, 2,000 feet high, we saw a panorama of countless cliffs of all sizes stretching down to Andeness, and opposite to us, the gloomy, rugged wastes of Norway, which show iron-bound walls, waterfalls, and bleak headlands, without woods, meadows, or habitations. For many hours we were mocked by an eagle, which, now soaring high, now darting down with rapid flight, gave his unwieldy pursuers a stiff and exhausting climb. We at last put to sea on the 26th of June, and passed the enormous rocky pile of Fugloe, down the precipitous face of which the inhabitants descend by means of ropes to get the down of the Eider-geese. Next day we were out of sight of land. The breeze freshened, and, as we sailed further to the north, we saw many whales. On

the 28th of June we came on the *first ice*—a sight which reminds the Polar navigator that he has reached his home! Driven down by the north wind, its fragments lay thickly on the misty horizon like gleaming points. We were now south-east of Bear Island in 73° 40′ N. Lat. and 21° E. Long., and found the ice so broken up that we did not hesitate to penetrate it, in order to find out the latitude in which its closed masses would appear. We passed through forty miles of this loose drift-ice, and then came on the pack in 74° 30′ N. Lat. and 23° E. Long. Already, on the 30th of June we had experienced the powerlessness of a small sailing vessel in such circumstances. The calms which had set in rendered it impossible to steer the ship, just when the ice was drifting in wild confusion. In spite of all our efforts to warp, the ship was inclosed by ice—in fact, *beset*. During our captivity of ten days, there was an alternation of fogs and gales with heavy sea-swells. The neighbourhood of floes, sometimes small, sometimes large, which constantly shifted their places, kept us in a state of continual watchfulness. The *Isbjörn*, on some of these days, sustained such severe pressures from the ice, that her safety was imperilled. On the 4th of July we had heavy storms from the South-east, which packed the ice still closer,

and, though the sea is generally quite calm within the
ice, it was otherwise on this occasion. In the afternoon
we heard through the dense fog the thunder of the
ocean breaking on the outer edge of the ice, and the
roar increased as the sea rose. Our attempts to haul
further into the ice and still-water were fruitless; the
ship was pressed too firmly, and was not to be moved
from its place. Our position became more and more
critical as the sea continued to rise. During the whole
night the waves roared and boiled around us. The
rudder groaned under the pressure of the floes, and had
to be made fast to prevent its being broken off. A
mass of ice grazing past the davits utterly destroyed one
of our boats. The critical nature of such a situation is
simply the uncertainty as to the amount of pressure,
which a ship can sustain. Towards evening the fog
lifted and rolled away, presenting a spectacle of fearful grandeur. All round us lay the open sea dashing
against the ice, which was itself in wild motion. Floes
and icebergs were driven about by the waves, and their
fragments strewed in all directions. At midnight our
little ship sustained shock after shock, and her timbers
strained and creaked. The "brash" of the crushed ice,
which had gathered round the ship, prevented her destruction. As the storm abated, the larger masses of

ice moved off to the edge of the horizon, so that in the morning we could not see open water from the deck. The day broke: what a change in the ice! The sea was calm, and a long swell died out on its outer edge. Piles of ice all round us,—a weird and death-like calm! The heavens were cloudless; the countless blocks and masses of ice stood out against the sky in blue neutral shadow, and the more level fields between them sparkled like silver as they shone in the sun. The movement of the sea beyond the ice abated, "leads" within the floes, hitherto scarcely perceptible, widened out. But again the sky was over-cast, the sea assumed the colour of lead, though it continued quite calm and the "ice-blink" appeared on the northern horizon.

9. On the 10th of July the ship under full sail forced her way through the floes, which were still somewhat close, and reached open water. The masses of ice through which we pressed were of considerable size. We now continued our course, which had been interrupted in the manner described, along the ice-barrier in a north-easterly direction. After leaving the Norwegian coast, the depth of the sea decreased considerably. We were now on the bank of Bear Island, and we found bottom at 90 metres (49·213 fathoms). Our course was impeded by

calms, currents and winds from the East, and even in the middle of July by severe storms. We were sometimes in drift-ice and sometimes outside of it. We soon discovered, that the ice of these seas was not to be compared with the vast masses of the Greenland seas. The floes we saw were not more than one year old. As we sailed eastward, the icebergs were neither so numerous nor so large, and disappeared almost entirely at 40° E. Long., which we reached on the 21st of July, after we had followed the ice-barriers from 74° to 75° 30′ N. Lat. Here we penetrated within them. Though drift-ice lay on every side, a steamer would have found nothing to arrest her progress. But the prevalence sometimes of east winds, sometimes of calms, the constant occurrence of fogs, the defects of our vessel, the little authority we had over the crew, when extraordinary labour was demanded, the great extent of the region to be explored,—all these difficulties prevented our pressing on in this direction. We therefore turned, July 22, in a westerly direction, in order to explore another opening in the ice, into which we advanced for about fifteen miles, and found floes not more than a year old lying so loosely together, that our ship under full sail seemed to pass over them, much in the same fashion as a sledge glides over a snow-covered plain. But again our course had to be altered, and Weyprecht steered the vessel in a south-westerly direction to the ice-barrier. In 76° 30' N. Lat. and 29° E. Long. we came on high and close masses of ice, and escaped with much difficulty (July 29) the danger of being again " beset."

10. We had meantime been convinced that, though the state of the ice was on the whole so favourable, we could not, with the means at our command and with a crew not trained to habits of obedience, do more than carry out our original intention. We could not make up for the defects of our sailing craft by any special exertion on the part of the crew. Could we have done this, we might have penetrated further in a northerly direction; though at this late period of the summer, we could not calculate on being able to return, and by the end of October our provisions would have been exhausted. We could only, therefore, attempt to reach Gillis' Land, and ascertain, whether it possessed the importance attributed to it by the Swedes. A safe harbour had therefore to be sought, in which the ship might be left, while a party in a boat should make for the mysterious land. Such a harbour we expected to find at Cape Leigh-Smith. We therefore held to the westward, towards the Stor-Fiord. It is an extremely hazardous thing, demanding incessant

attention, to tack and cruise at the ice-barrier during the continuance of fogs and with heavy seas and unfavourable winds. Not unfrequently, the ice-blink is seen all round the horizon, and we discover that we have come into a great "ice-hole," or a calm makes it impossible to steer the ship, just when a strong current is bearing her into the thickest of the ice-masses. We had our share of these and other risks till we suddenly beheld, while sailing in a fog among icebergs a hundred feet high, the long stretching plateau of Hope Island. According to Weyprecht's observations, there is an error of 40' in latitude in the position of this island on the Swedish maps. The real position of the south-west cape of Hope Island is 76° 29' N. Lat., and 25° E. Long. Seduced by a great opening in the ice, and deviating from our course for a short time, we advanced in a northerly direction to the east of the island, in the hope of reaching Gillis' Land from thence. But after sailing in a fog for a whole day among icebergs lying close to the cliffs of the island, we were driven further westward, and coming suddenly on the ice—Lat. 76° 30'—with an exceedingly high sea, escaped being dashed to pieces as by a miracle. To penetrate here was an impossibility. We therefore altered our course again for Walter-Thymen's Straits. A dense girdle of ice several miles deep, and a strong current setting towards the south-west, frustrated every attempt to land on Hope Island. To the west of this we found the ice-barrier in 76° N. Lat., formed of heavy pack-ice, and small icebergs. Our passage to the South Cape (Cape Look-out) of Spitzbergen (76° 30′ N. Lat.) was comparatively quick. Numerous cliffs and rocks on which the waves were breaking, not marked on any chart, rose in the night of August 4 out of the fog at the distance of a few ships' lengths from us, and it was with the utmost difficulty that we could tack with the heavy sea and strong north-east wind.

11. The day after, when the heavy storm-clouds lifted from the table-land of Cape Look-out, we made the unpleasant discovery, that we were to the south-west of it. Hitherto we had been sailing in dense fog, but after passing this Cape we had almost unbroken sunshine, which illuminated the whole western side of Spitzbergen up to Prince Charles's foreland. A current one or two miles wide, which flows southward, turns at Cape Look-out and flows in a northerly direction. At this Cape, which is the apex of the current, besides many rocks on which the waves break, there are twenty islands, some of them of considerable size. This promontory, which has been of great importance to navigators for more than 200 years,

is erroneously represented in the charts I have seen. Many ships, therefore, have been wrecked at this place, chiefly those of the Spitzbergen whalers and sealers, who base their sailing on making this headland, though they are ignorant of its exact geographical position. Thrice we tried at the beginning of August to reach the Stor-Fiord from the western side of Cape Look-out, and thrice we were driven back by this current, though the wind was in our favour. This, however, gave us an opportunity we had not expected, of seeing something of the west coast of Spitzbergen with its fiords and glaciers as far as Horn Sound. A fog, as dense as coal smoke, floats almost always over "Horn-sundstind" (4,500 feet high) and the pyramid of Haytand. The slopes, clothed in dull green, running down to the coast, make Spitzbergen seem scarcely an Arctic land, when compared with the cold grandeur of Greenland. The rocky shores of the northern parts of Norway are more dreary, and wear more the aspect of Arctic regions than Spitzbergen. Hence General Sabine, comparing Spitzbergen with Greenland, called it "a true paradise."

12. On the 10th of August the ice began to move out from the Stor-Fiord. It pushed on with great velocity from the north-east, turned round Cape Look-out, and deposited itself along the west coast, covering it with

thick layers in sixteen hours. On the 12th of the month, in consequence of the fog and strong current, we found ourselves between the heavy drift ice and the reefs of Cape Look-out. According to our reckoning we should have been twenty-five miles to the east of it. It was only by boldly charging the drift-ice, with the vessel under full sail, that the *Isbjörn* escaped the danger of being beset. On the 13th the wind chopped round, and, standing away to the south, we succeeded, after cruising about for ten days, in running into Wyde Jans Water. Our involuntary detention off Cape Look-out enabled us to land twice. During one of these visits we built a cairn, in which we deposited a notice of the course we had steered. The hasty survey we made enabled us to correct some very gross errors in the maps. On the evening of the 14th we sighted Edge Island, and cruised in the drift-ice, which was becoming gradually more dense in that direction. Here we fell in with two ships from Finland, engaged in the capture of the walrus, and learnt from their skippers some particulars concerning the state of the ice, which induced us to give up the direct course to Cape Leigh-Smith, and to prefer coasting along the west side of the Fiord.

13. The ice was now more packed. The ship, weakened by numerous ice-pressures and countless shocks, and

making much water, was in so bad a condition that part of the bows under the water-line was shattered, and some timbers of the hull were forced in. In order to give some notion of the force of the shocks to which we had been exposed in forcing our course through the ice, let it suffice to say, that the iron plating an inch thick with which the bows had been strengthened at Tromsoe, had been broken off like so many chips.

14. Tacking up against the north wind we came, in the night of August 16, on broken ice off Whale's Bay, in 77° 30′ N. Lat. The expected free coast-water was not to be found, and the prevailing winds from the north took away any hope of reaching Cape Leigh-Smith in less than a week. Our plan of a boat expedition, for which three weeks would have been necessary, from Cape Leigh-Smith to explore Gillis' Land had now to be renounced; and as the southern extremity of Stor-Fiord is generally blocked up at the end of August by an accumulation of ice brought from the east, we were constrained to leave the fiord at once, and return to the ice-barrier we had left.

15. The geological formation of the western coast of this fiord has never been explored. From a visit to the land and the ascent of a mountain 2,000 feet high, we learnt some interesting facts concerning its Jurassic formation, which appeared to extend far to the south.

We found traces, at some distance apart, of the more recent brown coal, and fossil remains (Bivalves in ferruginous chalk-marl) ; we gathered also some plants still in flower, and brought away some red snow. This excursion enabled us also to examine the beautifully-developed glaciers of Spitzbergen. Hornsundtind (4,500 feet high) is a most imposing mountain, and viewed from the east resembles a sugar-loaf. The other mountains on the coast of the fiord rise to heights varying from 2,000 to 4,000 feet. Noble glaciers slope down both sides of the main ridge, which runs in a southerly direction through the island. Some of these, when they reach the sea, are three or four miles wide, and their terminal fronts are about 80 feet high. The snow-line of those which debouch on the Stor-Fiord is at an altitude of 1,000 feet, and their surface is little broken by crevasses. None of these glaciers are of sufficient size to shed icebergs, properly speaking. The sea close to the coast is shallow, and the detachments from the glaciers are merely larger or smaller blocks of ice.

16. On the evening of August 16, sailing before the wind, we forced our way through the ice of the Stor-Fiord, and two days afterwards arrived at Hope Island, the steep, rocky walls of which, rose out of the fog just as we were close under it. We found the icebergs still firmly grounded, precisely as we had observed

them three weeks before. As an unusually strong current was running towards the south-west at the rate of two miles an hour, great caution was needed when we landed in the whale-boat amid rocks and cliffs, not marked on any chart. The geological formation of the island was identical with that of the mountainous region on the south of Whale's Bay. We found brown coal, but the shortness of our visit did not permit us to inspect the beds of it. Drift wood of Siberian larch and pine lay in great quantities on the shore.

17. It was surprising to observe the change which meanwhile had taken place; the ice both to the west and east of us had disappeared. We were eager to find it, and again penetrated as far as possible into it. We tacked about on the 19th, 20th, and 21st of August—the weather being stormy—with little success against the north wind, which had prevailed for some weeks. A current from the north drove us constantly southwards. After leaving the Stor-Fiord the temperature of the water exceeded the temperature of the air. On the 22nd of August, in 76° 45′ N. Lat. and 28° 30′ E. Long. we found very little drift-ice, which standing out but a few inches above the water level presented no impediment to navigation. Nothing but contrary winds stood in the way of our penetrating in a northerly direction, except, indeed, the doubts and fears raised by our skipper and

his crew at our attempting higher latitudes at so late a period of the year. König Karl's Land lay only forty miles to the north—still invisible on account of the mists. Fresh traces of Polar bears announced the neighbourhood of land. We therefore bore away to the east in 32° E. Long. on the 24th of August—the day on which the sun set for the first time. The number of icebergs constantly increased from this date, while some weeks previously, in the same region, we had scarcely seen one. This, perhaps, is to be explained from the fact, that their appearance is irregular, depending on the varying movement of the glaciers, and also on the time and manner in which the icebergs clear out from the bays and fiords. On the 26th we had stormy weather, rain, and snow. On the 27th, amid a dense fog, and with the sea running high, we came close to an iceberg, against which the sea was dashing itself in foam and spray, just in time to avert a collision. On the 29th of August we perceived that the ship had been carried 1° 30′ eastward in a short time by a current. The further we sailed in this easterly direction, the further northward the ice retreated, and we began to hope that we should come nearer the Pole than any ship ever had in this sea. The southern limit of the ice-barrier in the Novaya Zemlya seas, towards the end of summer, is usually placed at 76° N. Lat., but we had reached 78° N. Lat., with 42° E. Long., without seeing (August 30th) a fragment of ice. The *Isbjörn* had, therefore, penetrated 100 miles in seas hitherto unknown. There was still a long heavy swell from the north, but the temperature of the water had fallen 2° within twenty-four hours, and it was no longer of an ultramarine, but of a dirty green colour; so that, notwithstanding the sanguine expectations we had cherished, we expected every moment to come on pack-ice. Already, too, the "ice-blink" was visible here and there on the horizon.

18. Whales, secure from persecution in this remote sea, seemed to abound; we saw many "blowing" and spouting. They came sometimes in pairs close to the ship. Their chase and capture might have been carried on here with every hope of success. On the morning of the 31st of August we saw six Eider-geese, the precursors of near land. A blue shadow on the eastern sky arrested the attention of us all for a long time. We felt as if we were on the brink of great discoveries. But, alas! the supposed land dissolved into mist. The poverty of our equipment prevented us from penetrating further. We might easily have been driven onwards by unknown currents, and the ice closing behind us might have cut off return to Europe. We could not

be assured that we not had come upon a bight, or *cul-de-sac*, stretching far to the north, and which might quickly change its character. On the night of August 31st, in 78° N. Lat., the ice lay in some places loose and widely dispersed, in others it was more compact, but nowhere was it in great masses; it scarcely rose above the horizon, and it was entirely without icebergs. There was nothing to prevent a vessel with steam power from penetrating further.

19. Still following the ice-barrier as it retreated northwards, we passed beyond 78° 30′ N. Lat. in the night of August 31st. The influence of the high latitudes we had reached, on the duration of light, was unmistakable. For some days, however, the temperature had fallen below zero (R.), a coating of snow lay on the deck, and the rigging was covered with ice like glass. The morning of the 1st of September broke; about half-past three o'clock fresh breezes from the north drove off the mist, and revealed one of those pictures peculiar to the high north from its dazzling effects of colour—the beams of the sun in glowing splendour were piercing through heavy masses of clouds, while the moon shone on the opposite side of the heavens. An ice-blink resembling an Aurora lay on the north.

20. We had reached 78° 38′ N. Lat., and yet the ice around us presented no serious impediment—none at

least as far as we could see. Should we then venture further with our ship in its weakened condition? We might still follow up an opening within the ice running northward, though, in doing this, we should expend the time needed for the exploration of the eastward-lying Novaya Zemlya seas. We determined therefore to bear away to the east before some currents of loose drift-ice. But fog and a high sea from the north-west caused us to alter our course more and more to the south-east. For the first time in these high latitudes we observed drift-wood, and we found ourselves in a sea, the temperature of which at the surface, did not materially exceed the temperature of the air. Whenever, however, the temperature of the air rose, a thaw suddenly set in. The colour of the sea alternated between blue and a dull green. A few days previously we had passed over a sea extraordinarily rich in the ribbed Medusæ (Beroë), and where the Rorqual (whale) abounded.

21. The great question now arose, whether the open water found in these high latitudes were only an accidental bight in the ice or a connected sea. It seemed bold to assume the latter, since 76° 30′ N. Lat. had never before been passed in that region. In order, therefore, to arrive at some positive conclusion on this point, we stood away from the ice at noon of the 1st of September, and ran down in open water to 75° 52′ N. Lat. and 51

44′ E. Long., intending to return to the north again, in order to explore the state of the ice to the north-east. Overcoming with much difficulty the opposition of our skipper, we returned to the edge of the ice, which we found, September 5th, in 78° 5′ N. Lat. and 56° E. Long. Though there was not much wind, a high sea running on the ice compelled us to leave it. In our course to the south-east we crossed 77° 30′ N. Lat. and 59° E. Long; here, also, to the south of 78°, there was no ice. To penetrate further to the east formed no part of our plan, and since another attempt to return to the ice would have been objectless, for the reasons above stated, we proposed to run into a bight on the west coast of Novaya Zemlya to take in fuel and water, which we urgently needed. The longer nights now made it almost impossible to manœuvre a ship in the ice when the winds were high, though a good steamer might have persisted for some time longer. The temperature of the sea on the 5th of September was +3° R. in Lat. 77° 30′, and on the 8th of the month, when we were in sight of Cape Nassau, it reached +4°.

22. Storms compelled us to keep to sea. As a current constantly set us to the north-east, we found it not possible to land in Novaya Zemlya, scarcely even to see it. On the night of September 12th we came into the region where the equatorial and Polar air-currents

meet, and had an opportunity of observing the hurricane like effects of their conjunction. The barometer fell about two inches, and the sea was so broken that the ship could hardly be steered, even with a fresh wind. On September 14th we were off Matoschkin Schar, and could not anchor, a snowstorm from the north-east completely hiding the coast. The change, which meantime had taken place in the sky, was strange and remarkable. Heavy thunder-clouds lay over our heads, just as they do in the region of the trade-winds, and every moment threatened to discharge themselves. On the 13th of September we saw the first Aurora, in the shape of an arch, passing through our zenith. The want of fuel and water, from which we began to suffer, and the end of the season for navigation, compelled us to avail ourselves of the favourable wind which had set in, and begin our voyage home, without landing on Novaya Zemlya. On this same day three of our crew of seven men, fell ill, one of them with scurvy. A heavy storm from the north-east compelling us to heave to, we lay close under the coast of Lapland for a whole day. On the 20th of September we ran into Tana Fiord on the east of North Cape, the most northerly point of Europe, and took in water. The gloomy cliffs of Tanahorn and the rocky iron-bound coasts were not at all behind the lands we had left in their terrible desolation. On the 24th of August the *Isbjörn* passed North Cape; on the 4th of October she anchored in Tromsoe. Weyprecht had remained on board while, with a Lapland sailor, who could speak Norwegian, I left the ship in Tana Fiord and went on to Tromsoe through Lapland, sometimes by means of a small boat on the shallow rivers and sometimes by means of reindeer sledges.

23. It had formed no part of our plan, either to make discoveries, or to reach high latitudes. Our object was to investigate, whether the Novaya Zemlya seas offered greater facilities, either from the influence of the Gulf Stream, or from any other causes, for penetrating the unexplored Polar regions. Many arguments, derived from the scientific results of our voyage, would seem to favour this idea, and in contradiction to the discouraging views of our predecessors, whose failures are explained by their defective equipment and the choice of the most unfavourable season for navigation, we ventured to draw the following inferences:

(1.) The Novaya Zemlya Sea is not filled with impenetrable ice, rendering navigation impossible; on the contrary, it is open every year, probably up to 78° of N. Lat., and is connected with the Sea of Kara, which is also free from ice in autumn, and even, it may be, with the "Polynjii," in the North of Asia. If this inference should not be admitted, the following remarks of Lieutenant Weyprecht, in anticipation of objections, are put forward as worthy of consideration:—" In all probability the open condition of the ice in 1871 will be ascribed to chance, or to an especially favourable ice-year. With respect to the latter alternative, the accounts given by the Walrus-hunters of Spitzbergen and Novaya Zemlya, should convince us, that the year 1871 was, not only, not a favourable, but a most unfavourable year in the ice. It was almost impossible to navigate Wibe-Jans Water, and the Sea of Kara could only be reached through the most southerly straits—the Jugorsky Straits. There remains, therefore, only the other objection, that the accident of favourable winds was the cause of our penetrating so far. But our meteorological journal shows North, or at any rate Northerly winds, and often, too, blowing freshly, from August 4th to September 5th, with the exception of twelve watches, *i.e.*, two days. But in no case could these winds have driven the ice to the north. With respect to the loose character of the ice we encountered, it might be said, that we saw only the outer ice. But, in the first place, we were often so far within the barrier that it would be inadmissible to speak of it as the outer ice; and, in the second place, the ice-barrier shows the state of the ice behind it. Whenever the wind lies against the ice, there the ice is always the most dense and packed, and we find open places only when we have worked our way through the outer ice."

(2.) The time most favourable for navigation in this sea falls at the end of August, and lasts—though rendered hazardous by storms, the formation of young ice, and the darkness which supervenes at that season—till the end of September, and during this period the ice may be said to be at its minimum.

(3.) The Novaya Zemlya Sea is a shallow sea,—a connection and continuation of the great plains of Siberia. In the extreme north, its depth was 180 metres, and south-east of Gillis' Land about 90 metres.

(4.) Gillis' Land is not a continent, but either an island or a group of islands. Whereas, from the circumstance that in the highest latitudes—in 79° N. Lat.—we found drift-wood covered with mud, sea-weed, creatures which live only near the land, decreasing depths of the sea, sweet-water ice and icebergs laden with dirt, it may be inferred, with great probability, that there exist masses of land to the north-east of Gillis' Land.

(5.) The appearance of Siberian drift-wood, only in the most northern seas reached in our voyage, seems to point to an easterly current there.

(6.) The Russian expeditions in the past and present centuries, which attempted to penetrate by the north-west coast of Novaya Zemlya, miscarried, because they sailed before the favourable season for navigation, and also because they had not the advantage of steam.

(7.) How far the Gulf Stream has any share or influence in the favourable conditions for the navigation of the Eastern Polar Sea which have been described, cannot as yet be positively determined. The state of the ice, the observations which were made on the temperature of the sea, its colour and the animal life found in it, seem to speak in favour of the action of this current in that region. It is possible that the Gulf Stream may exercise its culminating influence on the west coast of Novaya Zemlya only at the beginning of September; for while the temperature of the sea in the months of July and August gradually fell from $+6°$ to $+2°$ in Lat. 75° N., and to zero and below it, still more to the north, we observed $+3°$ R., September 6, in Lat. 78°, and $+4°$ R., September 10, in Lat. 75° 30′. The temperature of the air was in all these cases considerably less than that of the water. If the unusually favourable state of the ice on the east of Spitzbergen should be ascribed to warm southerly currents of air, it may be replied that our observations specify the almost uninterrupted occurrence of north winds. It is also possible, that at the beginning and middle of summer the Gulf Stream may move slowly in a northerly direction along the coasts of Novaya Zemlya, and that towards autumn it spreads itself more and more to the west. Our observations proved the existence, in the eastern Novaya Zemlya seas, of a band of warm water, from thirty-six to forty feet deep, beneath which lies, without gradation, a colder stratum. It is evident that the unequal density of these strata prevents their mingling. This band of warmer water near North Cape is about 150 feet deep, with a temperature of nearly $+ 7°$ C., but diminishes as it flows northward. The frequency of fogs and mists in the Novaya Zemlya Sea, and the squalls unknown to other Arctic regions, which are characteristic of a more southerly region, indicate also a current of warm water. How this warm current gradually cools towards the north, and becomes shallower, and how distinctly it divides into those strata of water of equal temperature, so characteristic of the Gulf Stream, is shown by three series of observations taken by Weyprecht at different latitudes, with the maximum and minimum thermometer of Casella :—

72° 30′ lat., 44° long.	77° 26′ lat., 44° long.	76° 40′ lat., 55° long.
12 to 114′ $+$ 4·8° C.	6′ to 30′ $+$ 2·2° C.	6′ to 36′ $+$ 2·5 C.
144 $+$ 2·5	36 $+$ 1·8	48 $+$ 1·0
174 $+$ 2·0	45 $+$ 0·3	60 $-$ ·0
204 $+$ 1·5	60 $+$ 0·3	72 - 0·6
234 $+$ 1·3	75 $-$ 0·9	90 $-$ 0·6
264 $+$ 1·0	90 $-$ 0·8	120 1·3
294 $+$ 0·5	120 $-$ 1·6	180 $-$ 1·2
360 $+$ 0·5	180 $-$ 1·8	300 1·2
450 $+$ 0·0	360 $-$ 1·6	
600 $-$ 0·4		
800 $-$ 1·3		

24. These inferences rendered the despatch of a well-equipped expedition to the Novaya Zemlya seas very desirable, either to penetrate towards the north, or to pursue the direction of the north-east passage. To this idea a most gracious reception was given by the Emperor of Austria. Hence arose the Austro-Hungarian expedition of 1872. The promoters of this undertaking assumed neither the existence of an open Polar Sea, nor the possibility of reaching the Pole by sledge or boat expeditions. Their object, simply and broadly stated, was the exploration of the still unknown Arctic regions, and it was their belief, that a vessel could penetrate further into this region by the route between Novaya Zemlya and Spitzbergen, where the *Isbjörn* in her pioneer voyage found the ice more loose and navigable than had been imagined possible. But in addition to the causes already specified, the influence of the warm currents, produced by the great rivers of Siberia discharging themselves into a shallow sea, was also supposed to co-operate in producing this phenomenon. Of these rivers, the Obi and Jenisej alone discharge into that shallow sea a body of water as great as the waters of the Mediterranean or the waters of the Mississippi. The course of the current produced by these mighty rivers is as yet unknown; but it was natural to suppose, that old and heavy pack-ice could not be formed on a coast

submitted to such an influence. This is confirmed by the observations of the Russians, who in the coldest period of the year always find open water in the Siberian seas. Middendorf, August 26, 1844, found the Gulf of Taimyr quite free from ice; our own observations, made in 60° E. Long., and those of the Norwegian Mack, who advanced to 81° E. Long. (75° 45′ N. Lat.), support the supposition of a still navigable sea. Of the region between Cape Tscheljuskin and the ice-free spaces asserted to exist by Wrangel, and others, we know but little; but it is probable, that the character of the ice in those seas does not greatly differ from the character of the ice in contiguous seas. Of the seas between Novaya Zemlya and Behring's Straits, at the distance of a few miles from the Asiatic coast, nothing is known. No ship has ever navigated this enormous Eastern Polar Sea.

25. It was the plan of the Austro-Hungarian expedition to penetrate in an E.N.E. direction, in the latter half of August, when the north coast of Novaya Zemlya is generally free from ice. The places at which the expedition was to winter were left undetermined; these might, possibly, be Cape Tscheljuskin, the new Siberian islands, or any lands which might be discovered. A return to Europe through Behring's Straits, however improbable it might be, lay among the possibilities of

the venture. Minor details were left to circumstances. In the event of the loss of the ship, the expedition was to endeavour to reach the coast of Siberia by boats, and, on one of the gigantic water-courses of Northern Asia, penetrate into more southern regions. The depôt of provisions and coals which it was Graf Wilczek's intention to deposit on the north coast of Novaya Zemyla, was to be the nearest refuge for the crew in the event of disaster to the ship. Stone cairns were to be erected on all prominent localities, and in these were to be laid accounts of the course of the expedition. Till its return at the end of the autumn of 1874, its members were to be cut off from all intercourse with Europe. The motives of an undertaking so long and so laborious cannot be found in the mere love of distinction or of adventure. Next to the wish to serve the interests of science by going beyond the footsteps of our predecessors, we were influenced by the duty of confirming and fulfilling the hopes which we ourselves had excited.

VOYAGE OF THE "TEGETTHOFF."
JUNE, 1872—SEPTEMBER, 1874.

I.
FROM BREMERHAVEN TO KAISER FRANZ-JOSEF LAND.

CHAPTER I.

FROM BREMERHAVEN TO TROMSOE.

1. HE who seeks to penetrate the recesses of the Polar world chooses a path beset with toils and dangers. The explorer of that region has to devote every energy of mind and body to extort a slender fragment of knowledge from the silence and mystery of the realm of ice. He must be prepared to confront disappointments and disasters with inexhaustible patience, and pursue devotedly his object, even when he himself becomes the sport of accident. That object must not be the admiration of men, but the extension of the domain of knowledge. He spends long years in the most dreadful of all banishments, far from his friends, from all the enjoyments of life, surrounded by manifold perils, and bearing the burden of utter loneliness. The grandeur therefore, of his object can alone support him,—for otherwise the dreary void of things without can only be an image of the void within. How many are the preconceptions with which the novice begins the voyage to the rugged, inclement

north! Books can tell him little of the stern life to which he dooms himself, as soon as he crosses the threshold of the ice, thinking perhaps to measure the evils that await him by the physical miseries of cold instead of by the moral deprivations in store for him.

2. In the year 1868, while employed on the survey of the Ortelcr Alps, a newspaper with an account of Koldewey's first expedition one day found its way into my tent on the mountain side. In the evening I held forth on the North Pole to the herdsmen and *Jägers* of my party as we sat round the fire, no one more filled with astonishment than myself, that there should be men endued with such capacity to endure cold and darkness. No presentiment had I then, that the very next year I should myself have joined an expedition to the North Pole; and as little could Haller, one of my *Jägers* at that time, foresee that he would accompany me on my third expedition. And much the same was it with the three and twenty men who early in the morning of June 13, 1872, came on board the vessel in Bremerhaven, to cast in their lot with the ship *Tegetthoff*, whatever that lot might be; for we had all bound ourselves by a formal deed, renouncing every claim to an expedition for our rescue, in case we should be unable to return. Our ideal aim was the north-east passage, our immediate and definite object was the

exploration of the seas and lands on the north-east of Novaya Zemlya.

3. A bright day rose with us, and no augur's voice could have heightened the glad hopes which animated every one of us. Friends from Austria and Germany had come to bid us a last farewell; but, as every venture should be, so our departure that morning was, quiet and without pretension. About six o'clock in the morning the *Tegetthoff* lifted her anchor and dropped down the *Schleusen* and the *Weser*, towed by a steamer. Down the broad stream we calmly glided, full of satisfaction at the fulfilment of long-cherished plans. There lay the same pastures, the same trees and meadows which had so delighted us on our return from Greenland. Yet unmoved we saw all the charms of nature grow young under the morning sun and then fade away in the evening twilight—as the land gradually disappeared behind us, and the coasts of Germany were lost to view. With the feeling that we were leaving them for so long a time, our thoughts turned to our new life in the narrow limits of a ship, and the resolve to live and labour in harmony animated each breast. How often we should be liable to casualties which no eye could foresee, we were soon to find out, when in almost dead calm and without steam we came on the shallow waters of Heligoland. What would have become of

the expedition, had we not discovered in time, that we had only a few feet of water under the keel!

4. The vessel, 220 tons burden, was fitted out for two years and a half, but was over-freighted by about thirty tons, so that our available space was much curtailed. Yet the cabin, which Weyprecht, Brosch, Orel, Kepes, Krisch, and I occupied, was far more commodious than the miserable hole in which eight of us had been crowded together on our Greenland expedition. Our supply of coals, 130 tons, was large in proportion to the size of the ship, being calculated not only for our daily wants, but to enable us to keep up steam for about sixty days. But to economise this store we used our sails, as much as possible, even in the ice. Both ship and engine— of 100 horse power—tested in the trial trip of June 8, sustained their character during the expedition, and did great credit to the Tecklenborg firm.

5. The wind being unfavourable, it took us some time to cross the North Sea and reach the coast of Norway. My journal describes this part of our voyage. "Light winds from the south carried the *Tegetthoff* on her lonely course over the North Sea. In undimmed brightness the blue sky stretched overhead, the air was balmy and mild. In the grey distance frowns the iron rampart of countless cliffs encircling the barren wastes of Norway. Occasionally a sea-gull comes near us, or

some bird rests on the mast-head; now and then a sail is seen on the horizon,—but save this, no life—no event. Every one feels, though no one utters it, that a grave future lies before him; each may hope what he wishes, for over the future there is drawn an impenetrable veil. All, however, are animated with the consciousness, that while serving science, we are also serving our Fatherland, and that all our doings will be watched at home with the liveliest sympathy.

"6. On board the *Tegetthoff* are heard all the languages of our country, German, Italian, Slavonic, and Hungarian; Italian, however, is the language in which all orders are given. The crew is lighthearted and merry: in the evening a gentle breeze carries the lively songs of the Italians over the blue sea, glowing under the midnight sun, or the monotonous cadence of the *Ludro* of the Dalmatians recalls the sunny home which they are so soon to exchange for its very opposite, which remains a sort of mystery to all their powers of fancy. Thus begins so peacefully our long voyage into the frozen ocean of the north. In a few weeks the ice will grate on the bows of the *Tegetthoff;* the crystal icebergs will surround her, and with many a strain will the good ship force her way through the icy wastes, sometimes inclosed on every side, sometimes free in coast-water, or threatened by the 'ice-blink' foreboding danger."

7. The officers and crew of the *Tegetthoff* amounted in all to twenty-four souls.

Lieutenant Carl Weyprecht, } *Commanders of the Expedition.*
Lieutenant Julius Payer,

Lieutenant Gustav Brosch,* } *Officers of the Ship.*
Midshipman Edward Orel,

Dr. Julius Kepes, *Physician to the Expedition.*
Otto Krisch, *Engineer.*
Pietro Lusina,† *Boatswain.*
Antonio Vecerina, *Carpenter.*
Josef Pospischill, *Stoker.*
Johann Orasch, *Cook.*
Johann Haller, } *Jägers, from Tyrol.*
Alexander Klotz,
Antonio Zaninovich, *Seaman.*
Antonio Catarinich, ditto.
Antonio Scarpa, ditto.
Antonio Lukinovich, ditto.
Giuseppe Latkovich, ditto.
Pietro Fallesich, ditto.
George Stiglich, ditto.
Vincenzo Palmich, ditto.
Lorenzo Marola, ditto.
Francesco Lettis, ditto.
Giacomo Sussich, ditto.
Captain Olaf Carlsen, *Icemaster and Harpooner.*

We had eight dogs on board; two we got in Lapland, the rest were brought from Vienna.

---

* Lieutenant Brosch had the entire care of the victualling department and deserved our heartiest thanks for the skill and self-sacrifice with which he performed this duty.

† Formerly Captain in the Austrian Merchant Service.

8. Stormy weather detained us for some time among the Loffoden Isles, so that we made Tromsoe only on July 3. Here we were received most courteously by the Austro-Hungarian Consul, Aagaard, who invited us to a banquet. We remained here a week, in order to complete our equipment. The ship, which had leaked considerably ever since we left Bremerhaven, was thoroughly examined by divers, the stores were landed, the ship repaired and reladen. Our supply of coals was replenished, a Norwegian whale-boat added to our equipment, and, lastly, the harpooner, Captain Olaf Carlsen, was taken on board. On July 6 we received our last news from Austria, letters and newspapers. The Ukase granted by the Russian Government also arrived, drawn up both for Weyprecht and myself in case of our being separated, a document of great importance, if the ship should be lost and we had to return through Siberia; an issue only too probable when the vast length and enormous difficulties of the north-east passage were considered. While Lieutenant Weyprecht was engaged in stopping the leak of the ship, some of us ascended—a Lapp of the name of Dilkoa being our guide—a pinnacle of rock, 4,000 feet high, towering over Tromsoe's labyrinth of fiords, in order to compare our aneroid and mercurial barometers. From the summit we beheld an enormous dark column of smoke rising perpendicularly to the

height of about 1,500 feet in the still air—the northern extremity of Tromsoe was in flames. Most gladly would we have learned something of the state of the ice this year; but as yet this was impracticable, for none of the walrus hunters had returned from their grounds in the north.

9. On the morning of Saturday, July 13, officers and crew heard mass from a French priest, and bidding adieu to our Tromsoe friends, we left the quiet little city, the most northerly of Europe, early on Sunday morning. The passengers of the Hamburg mail steamer, entering the harbour as we left it, greeted us with loud and long cheers, and steaming through the narrow Grötsound, close under the cliffs of Sandoe and Rysoe we came into the open sea, Captain Carlsen acting as our pilot. As we issued from the *Scheeren*, a mist arose which covered and obscured the huge rock of Fingloe. Here the engine fires were put out and the sails set, and the first and last voyage, which the *Tegetthoff* was destined to make, began. On July 15 we steered towards the north, the Norwegian coast with its many glaciers in full view, and on the 16th we sighted the North Cape in the blue distance.

CHAPTER II.

ON THE FROZEN OCEAN.

1. UNFAVOURABLE winds had hindered our progress for some days; we now encountered heavy seas. On July 23 a sudden fall of the temperature and dirty rainy weather told us that we were close to the ice, which we expected to find later and much more to the northward, and on the evening of July 25, lat. 74° 0' 15" N., we actually sighted it, the thermometer marking + 0°.2 and + 1° R. in the sea. The northerly winds, which had prevailed for some time, had broken up the ice, and it lay before us in long loose lines. Its outer boundary was consequently the very opposite of those solid walls of ice which we met with in Greenland in 1869, and two years afterwards, on the east of Spitzbergen. Though surprised at finding the ice so far to the south, we never imagined that this was anything but a collection of floes, which had drifted out perhaps from the Sea of Kara through the Straits of Matotschkin. But

only too soon the conviction was forced upon us that we were already within the Frozen Ocean, and that navigation in the year 1872 was to differ widely from that of the preceding year. Lieutenant Weyprecht had the day before fastened "the crow's-nest" to the mainmast of the *Tegetthoff*, and henceforth it became the abode of the officer of the watch. On July 26, while steering in a north-easterly direction, the ice became closer, though it was still navigable; but we nowhere saw the heavy fields which had astonished us on the east coast of Greenland, and which Lütke found to be so dangerous to navigation. The temperature of the air and the sea fell rapidly, and during the two following weeks it remained below the freezing point almost uniformly, and without any essential difference between day and night.

2. The frozen sea of Novaya Zemlya is characterized by that inconstancy of weather which in our lower latitudes we attribute to the month of April; the same variability is met with, though in lesser degree, in the Greenland seas during the summer months. Snowstorms now alternated with the most glorious blue skies. The black-bulbed thermometer showed $+ 36°$ R. in the sun, with $+ 3°$ R. in the shade. The hunting season began, and the kitchen was well provided with auks and seals. Our Dalmatians soon learnt to like the dark flesh of the latter.

SEAL LIFE IN THE FROZEN OCEAN.

3. The ice gradually became closer; July 29 (74° 44′ N. Lat., 52°8′ E. Long.) we were able to continue our course only under steam, and heavy shocks were henceforward inevitable; in many cases the vessel could not force a passage except by charging the ice. In the night a vast, apparently impenetrable barrier stopped our progress; but the tactics of charging under steam again cleared a passage, and we penetrated into a larger "icehole." We now glided along over the shining surface of its waters, as if we were navigating an inland lake, save that no copsewood clothed the shores, but pale blocks of ice, which the mist, that now fell and enveloped us, transformed into the most fantastic shapes, and at last into mere shapelessness itself. In all that surrounded us neither form nor colour was discernible; faint shadows floated within the veil of mist, and our path seemed to lead no whither. A few hours before the glowing fire of the noonday sun had lain on the mountain wastes of Novaya Zemlya, while refraction raised its long coast high above the icy horizon. Nowhere does a sudden change in Nature exercise so immediate an effect on the mind as in the Frozen Ocean, where, too, all that brings delight proceeds from the sun.

4. For some days we had entered into a world utterly strange to most of us on board the *Tegetthoff*. Dense mists frequently enveloped us, and from out of the mantle of

snow of the distant land the rocks, like decayed battlements, frowned on us inhospitably. There is no more melancholy sound than that which accompanies the decay and waste of the ice, as it is constantly acted on by the sea and thaw, and no picture more sad and solemn than the continuous procession of icebergs floating like huge white biers towards the South. Ever and anon there rises the noise of the ocean swell breaking amongst the excavations of the ice-floes, while the water oozing out from their icy walls falls with monotonous sound into the sea; or perhaps a mass of snow deprived of its support, drops into the waves, to disappear in them with a hissing sound as of a flame. Never for a moment ceases the crackling and snapping sound produced by the bursting of the external portions of the ice. Magnificent cascades of thaw water precipitate themselves down the sides of the icebergs, which sometimes rend with a noise as of thunder, as the beams of the sun play on them. The fall of the titanic mass raises huge volumes of foam, and the sea-birds, which had rested on its summit in peaceful confidence, rise with terrified screams, soon to gather again on another ice-colossus.

5. But what a change, when the sun, surrounded by glowing cirrus clouds breaks through the mist, and the blue of the heavens gradually widens out! The masses

of vapour, as they well up, recede to the horizon, and the cold ice-floes become in the sun-light dark borders to the "leads" which gleam between them, on the trembling surface of which the midnight sun is mirrored. Where the rays of the sun do not directly fall on it, the ice is suffused with a faint rosy haze, which deepens more and more as the source of light nears the horizon. Then the sunbeams fall drowsily and softly, as through a veil of orange gauze, all forms lose at a little distance their definition, the shadows become fainter and fainter, and all nature assumes a dreamy aspect. In calm nights the air is so mild that we forget we are in the home of ice and snow. A deep ultramarine sky stretches over all, and the outlines of the ice and the land tremble on the glassy surface of the water. If we pull in a boat over the unmoved mirror of the "ice-holes," close beside us a whale may emerge from its depths, like a black shining mountain; if a ship penetrates into the waste, it looks as weird as the "Flying Dutchman," and the dense columns of smoke, which rise in eddies from her funnel, remain fixed for hours until they gradually melt away. When the sun sinks at midnight to the edge of the horizon, then all life becomes dumb, and the icebergs, the rocks, the glaciers of the land glow in a rosy effulgence, so that we are hardly conscious of the desolation. The sun has reached its lowest point,—after a pause it begins to rise and gradually its paler beams are transformed into a dazzling brightness. Its softly warming light dissolves the ban under which congelation has placed nature, the icy streams, which had ceased to run, pour down their crystal walls. The animal creation only still enjoys its rest; the polar-bear continues to repose behind some wall of ice, and flocks of sea-gulls and divers sit round the edge of a floe, calmly sleeping with their heads under their wings. Not a sound is to be heard, save perhaps, the measured flapping of the sails of the ship in the dying breeze. At length the head of a seal rises stealthily for some moments from out the smooth waters; lines of auks, with the short quick beat of their wings, whiz over the islands of ice. The mighty whale again emerges from the depths, far and wide is heard his snorting and blowing, which sounds like the murmurs of a waterfall when it is distant, and like a torrent when it is near. Day reigns once more with its brilliant light, and the dreamy character of the spectacle is dissolved.

6. We had sailed over one "ice hole," and again a dense barrier of ice frowned on us; as we forced our way into it, the ice closed in all round us—we were "beset." The ship was made fast to a floe, the steam blown off, its hot breath rushing with a loud noise through the cold mist;

every open mesh in the net of water-ways was closed by the ice, which soon lay in such thick masses around us, that any one provided with a plank, might have wandered for miles in any direction he liked. July 30, the *Tegetthoff* remained fast in her prison; no current of water, nor any movement among the floes lying close to us was discernible; a dead calm prevailed, and mist hung on every side. On the following day we made vain efforts to break through a floe which lay on our bows. The calm still prevailed, Aug. 1 (74° 39' N. L. 53° E. L.), and no change was to be seen in the ice. Aug. 2, the crew began with hearty goodwill the toilsome work of warping, but with no success, the smallness of the floes hardly admitting of this manœuvre. In the evening of the same day it seemed as if a fresh breeze would set us free; but after we had gone on for a few cables' length, a great floe once more barred the route, while at the same time the wind fell. At length, when the ice became somewhat looser, we got up the engine fires, and in the following night broke through, under steam, a broad barrier of ice, which separated us from the open coast-water of Novaya Zemlya. In the morning of Aug. 3, we forced our way into coast-water, twenty miles broad, to the north of Matotschkin Scharr, and steered due north, the mountainous coasts still in sight. A belt of ice 105 miles broad lay behind us. The country greatly resembled Spitzbergen, and we observed with pleasure its picturesque glaciers and mountains rising to the height of nearly 3000 feet, though inconsiderable compared with the mountains of Greenland. Far and wide not a fragment of ice was to be seen, there was a heavy swell on, the air was unusually warm ($+ 4°$ R.), in the evening rain fell, and on Aug. 4 we had dense mists and driving snow storms, which forced us to keep to the west of Admiralty Peninsula. During the night of Aug. 6, the snow-storms were heavier than before, and the deck was quite covered. Towards the north and west very close ice was seen, and since the temperature of the air, even with the winds in the south-west, remained constantly below zero, it was evident, that the ice must stretch far in that direction also. Aug. 7, we ran on the white barriers to the west of Admiralty Peninsula, and far to the north, beyond a broad field of ice, refraction indicated open water and showed the forms of "Tschorny Nos" floating in the air. In the afternoon of Aug. 8 the ice in $75° 22'$ N. L. became so thick around us, that we were compelled to have recourse to steam-power; but the *Tegetthoff* even with this auxiliary was unable against a head wind to penetrate a broad strip of close ice, and banking up our fires, we determined to wait its breaking up. Close under the coast open water was again observed, and in it—a Schooner! Every one now hastened to write letters to his friends and relations, but the schooner, to which we meant to give our letters and despatches, by running into the heart of Gwosdarew Bay escaped the duty we had in store for it. About half past ten P.M. the wind had fallen and the ice began

GWOSDAREW INLET.

to open out, and we were able to continue our voyage under steam in a north-westerly direction. The sun lay before us, the clear mirror of distant "leads" glowed with a glorious carmine, the barriers of ice which lay between these "leads" appeared as stripes of violet, and only our immediate neighbourhood was pale and cold. The *Tegetthoff* laboured through the dense accumulation of floes and about midnight reached open water, and the steam was again blown off. Aug. 9, we sailed in coast-water perfectly free from ice, excepting the icebergs we encountered, some about forty feet high. These, generally, were so numerous and so small in size, that they were at once seen to be offshoots from the small glaciers of Novaya Zemlya as they plunge into the sea. Their surface was frequently covered with debris. Loose drift ice showed itself, Aug. 10, but the ship continued to steer between the floes towards the north. In the forenoon of that day we were again nearly " beset," but happily escaped that fate after four hours' warping. Aug. 11 our course was continued without impediment in a northerly direction through the loose drift-ice. The land, from which we had hitherto remained distant about eight or twelve nautical miles, now declined in height from three thousand to fifteen hundred or a thousand feet, and quickly lost its picturesque character. On the noon of Aug. 12, on account of a thick mist we made fast to a great floe, and were able to commence on it the training of the dogs to drag the sledges.

7. In the neighbourhood of the Pankratjew Islands, a ship suddenly and unexpectedly appeared on the horizon, and endeavoured to gain our attention by

discharges from a mortar, and by the hoisting of flags. How great was our astonishment and our joy when we beheld the Austro-Hungarian flag at the peak of the *Isbjörn*, and were able to greet Count Wilczek, Commodore Baron Sterneck, Dr. Höfer, and Mr. Burger half an hour afterwards on board the *Tegetthoff*. Coming from Spitzbergen in the *Isbjörn* (the ship of our precursory expedition of 1871) they had sighted us two days before. That in a sailing vessel, and without any sufficient equipment, they had succeeded in following and overtaking the *Tegetthoff*, which had penetrated so far with difficulty and by the aid of steam, was a proof both of skill and resolution. Their object was to establish a depot of provisions at Cape Nassau, at whatever personal risk to themselves. About two o'clock in the morning our guests returned to the *Isbjörn*, and both ships now sailed in company, and without meeting any hindrance in the ice-free coast-water, in a northerly direction. In the forenoon of Aug. 13, in 76° 18′ N. Lat., and 61° 17′ E. Long., we came upon closer ice, amid mist and stormy weather, and the two ships anchored to some firm land-ice two cable lengths from each other, about a mile from the land. Close to the south of us lay the Barentz Isles with their singularly formed hills, which the walrus hunters call by the somewhat gloomy name of "the three coffins." On our north an enormous iceberg rose in dazzling whiteness above a faintly glimmering field of ice, a harbinger of new countries—for its size forbade us to think, that it owed its origin to the glaciers of Novaya Zemlya. Continuous winds from the W.S.W., close ice, mist, downfalls of snow, the necessity of determining the geographical position of the depot of provisions which we had established, compelled us to lie for eight days before the Barentz Islands. The opportunity we thus had of putting our feet once more on the land was exceedingly agreeable. We made repeated visits to the shore with two dog-sledges, in company with Professor Höfer; and as his observations on the phenomena of the country are those of a distinguished geologist, I here insert those he has kindly placed at my disposal.

8. "The Barentz Isles are flat, girt with cliffs and separated by narrow straits from the coast, which rises up terrace on terrace. Its rocks consist of a black, very friable slate, frequently alternating with strata of mountain limestone of the carboniferous period, varying in breadth from one to ten *metres*. These strata are filled with a countless number of fossilized inhabitants of the sea, trilobites, mussels, brachiopodes, crinoides, corals, &c., which are utterly foreign to the Frozen Ocean as it now is, and whose cognates live only in warm seas.

9. "The animal world, therefore, buried in the lime-

stone of these islands is an indisputable proof that there was once, in these high latitudes, a warm sea, which could not possibly co-exist with such great glaciers as those which now immerse themselves in the seas of Novaya Zemlya. That portion of the earth, now completely dead and buried in ice, once knew *a period of luxuriant life*. In its sea there revelled a world of life, manifold and beautiful in its forms, while the land, as the discoveries on Bear Island and Spitzbergen prove, was crowded with gigantic palm-like ferns. This age of the earth's history is called the carboniferous period; it was the rich and fertile youth of the high north, which lived out its time more rapidly, than the southern zones, now in all their vigour and variety. If we compare the Fauna buried in the chalk formations of the Barentz Isles, with the contemporaneous Fauna which we know from the carboniferous formation of Russia, specially that of the Ural, we find a very remarkable agreement not only in their general character, but also in particular organisms. Many of the fossils of the carboniferous limestone of these high degrees of latitude ($76°-77°$) are found in analogous strata of the Ural, and are proved by the researches of Russian geologists to exist there as far as the fiftieth degree of latitude. Without stopping to insist on the great similarity between the stratification of Novaya Zemlya and the Ural—the former being the real continuation of the latter—we dwell here on the fact that in the carboniferous period there was a sea, which stretched from the fiftieth to the seventy-seventh degree of north latitude, *i.e.*, twenty-seven degrees, or 405 geographical miles, which was animated by the same Fauna, and which consequently must have presented the same relations, especially a like warm temperature. From these signs it would appear that the zones of climate now so decisively marked on the surface of the earth did not exist at the carboniferous period. The horizontal surface of the land leads us at the first to infer horizontal stratification; but we find the contrary to be the case; the marine deposits once horizontal, have been so raised at a later period that they are now vertical. Since the friable slate degrades rapidly, and the limestone layers very gradually, it may be assumed that the former wasting away leaves the limestone layers standing like walls between them—a thing which, in a small scale may often be elsewhere observed. If a glance at these buried fossils awakens in us an image, as in a dream, of a creation rich in organic forms, a glance at the present state of the Barentz Isles impresses us with the gloomiest feelings.

10. "Before us lies this small greyish brown fragment of the earth. The cold, level ground is covered with sharp-edged pieces of rock, which appear to be as it

were macadamised, so closely are they rammed together. Here and there, about a fathom's length from each other, lie brownish green masses, like mole hills. When we examine them more closely, each mass resolves itself into a vast number of small plants of the same species (*Saxifraga oppositifolia*), whose little stalks are covered with dark green leaves, which are alive, and also with brown leaves, which have been dead for years and years, but wither in the cold much more gradually than with us. From this small heap, tender rosy blooms raise their little heads, bidding defiance to the bitter snowy weather, which sweeps over the miserable plain. Another species of saxifrage (*Saxifraga cæspitosa*), with shorter stalks and yellowish white flowers, growing in thick clumps, forms, together with the first named variety and the more rarely appearing *Saxifraga rivularis*, the hardiest representatives of this family of plants so frequently found in the Polar regions. If to these we add *Draba arctica* with its little yellow flowers, forming in valleys large patches of sward, the yellow flowering poppy (*Papaver nudicaule*), and a rare willow (*Salix polaris*), which with some few leaves peeps forth from the soil, we have described the whole Flora of that desolate waste, in which a mere passing glance would scarce detect the existence of vegetable life among the debris of rocks and the heaps of snow. Mosses are found here and there in the moister fissures of rocks, and especially on the coast, where old drift wood, or the bones of whales or other animals, afford the nourishment they need, and in some places the mosses spread themselves out into small carpets. Lichens love to shelter under the clusters of the different kinds of saxifrage, though sometimes they are found by themselves. Of this class we will mention merely the so-called Iceland moss (*Cetraria islandica*), and a reindeer lichen (*Cladonia pyxidata*); the few other forms are nearly related to those mentioned, and belong to the so-called creeping lichens. One peculiarity of the Flora of the far north, which we have already mentioned, is their growth in clumps. Only thus can these tender organisms maintain their existence against the stern elements; and this, indeed, is a characteristic of all Arctic creation, which is seen in the animal world also, when its means of nourishment are hard to find. We will point only to the herds of reindeer, of lemmings, of walruses, of seals, &c., lastly to the vast flocks of birds; all of which illustrate the principle: *common danger begets common defence.*"

11. Our involuntary leisure at the Barentz Isles enabled us to make some precautionary preparations for our future contests with the ice; for a ship may be crushed by the ice and sink in a few minutes, as had

happened some days previously, not far from us, to the yachts *Valborg* and *Iceland*. Provisions and ammunition for four weeks were got ready, and each man was entrusted with a special service, if it should ever come to this extremity. To guard against the dreaded pressures of the ice, heavy beams were hung round the hull of the vessel, so that the pressure on the ship might be distributed over a larger surface, and the vessel itself be raised instead of crushed. Our space on deck, somewhat limited at first, had been considerably enlarged, although our numerous sledges, our stock of drift-wood, and the rudder which had been unshipped, formed inconvenient obstacles, while the chained-up dogs occasioned some unpleasant surprises to those who had not succeeded in gaining their affections. These poor animals, without protection, suffered much from the cold rough weather which now prevailed, though subsequently some provision was made for their comfort. Sumbu and Pekel, the two Lapland dogs, were the most hardy, and slept without stirring, even when they were completely covered with snow. It was only after a long and stout resistance that the dogs became accustomed to the flesh of seals; at first they growled at every one who offered it to them.

12. Aug. 14, we were threatened by the advance of an enormous line of pack-ice, which inclosed us in the little "docks" of the land-ice, and caused the *Isbjörn*

to heel over. In the evening a bear came near this vessel, which was shot by Professor Höfer and Captain Kjelsen. On the following day, with the help of the dogs and sledges, we removed over the land ice to "the Three Coffins" the provisions which were to form the depot: 2,000 lbs. of rye-bread in casks, 1,000 lbs. of pease-sausages in tin cases. These were deposited in the

FORMATION OF THE DEPOT AT "THE THREE COFFINS."

crevice of a rock and secured against the depredations of bears. We felt assured of the conscientiousness of Russian or Norwegian fishermen, that they would make use of these provisions only under the pressure of urgent necessity. This depot was intended to be the first place of refuge, in the event of the ship being lost.

13. Both ships were dressed with flags, and round one common table we celebrated the birthday,

Aug. 18, of the Emperor and King, Francis Joseph I. Aug. 19, we fetched some drift-wood from the land, and saw from a height an "ice-hole" stretching to the north at no great distance from the coast. As we returned to the ship we came across a bear,

THE "TEGETTHOFF" AND "ISBJÖRN" SEPARATE.

which, being assailed by so many hunters at once, took to flight. Aug. 20, some changes in the ice seemed to make navigation possible, and we forthwith went on board the *Isbjörn* to bid adieu to our friends. It was no common farewell. A separation to those who are themselves separated from the world moves the heart to its depths. But besides this, in bidding adieu to Count Wilczek, we felt how much we were indebted to him, as the man who had fostered the work we were about to undertake, who dreaded no danger while providing for our safety in the event of a catastrophe to the expedition. Our high-minded friend was at this moment the embodiment of our country, which honouring us with its confidence and trust, demanded that we should devote all our energies to the high objects of the expedition. Often afterwards did this adieu return to our memories. With a fresh wind from the north-east we passed the *Isbjörn* as we steamed towards the north, while this vessel, veiled in mist, soon disappeared from our eyes.

14. Our prospects, so far as the object of our expedition was concerned, had meantime not improved. To cross the Frozen Sea to Cape Tscheljuskin in the present year, was not to be dreamt of, and yet the thought of wintering in the north of Novaya Zemlya was positively intolerable. The navigable water was becoming narrower every day, and the ice seemed to increase in solidity, especially in the neighbourhood of the coast. In the afternoon of this day we ran into an "ice-hole," but in the night barriers of ice stopped our further progress. As usual, the ship was made fast to a floe, the steam blown off,

and we awaited the parting asunder of the ice.[1] Five walruses who had been watching us from a rock as we entered that ill-starred "ice-hole," sprang into the water and disappeared.

15. Ominous were the events of that day, for immediately after we had made fast the *Tegetthoff* to that

THE "TEGETTHOFF" FINALLY BESET.

floe, the ice closed in upon us from all sides and we became close prisoners in its grasp. No water was to be seen around us, and *never again were we destined to see our vessel in water.* Happy is it for men, that

[1] Our position was then in 76° 22′ N. Lat., 63° 3′ E. Long.

inextinguishable hope enables them to endure all the
vicissitudes of fate, which are to test their powers of endurance, and that they can never see, as at a glance, the
long series of disappointments in store for them! We
must have been filled with despair, had we known that
evening, that we were henceforward doomed to obey the
caprices of the ice, that the ship would never again
float on the waters of the sea, that all the expectations
with which our friends, but a few hours before, saw the
Tegetthoff steam away to the north, were now crushed:
*that we were in fact no longer discoverers, but passengers
against our will on the ice.* From day to day we hoped
for the hour of our deliverance! At first we expected it
hourly, then daily, then from week to week; then at the
seasons of the year and changes of the weather, then
in the chances of new years! *But that hour never
came,* yet the light of hope, which supports man in all
his sufferings, and raises him above them all, never
forsook us, amid all the depressing influence of expectations cherished only to be disappointed.

CHAPTER III.

DRIFTING IN THE NOVAYA ZEMLYA SEAS.

1. AT the end of August the temperature in the Frozen Ocean is generally at the freezing point of the Centigrade thermometer, but this year (1872) it was constantly six degrees below it. A cold bleak air enveloped us, there was abundance of snow, the sun showed himself rarely, - and for some days he had sunk, at midnight, under the horizon. The ship and her rigging were stiff with ice, and everything indicated that for us winter had begun. As the masses of ice which inclosed us consisted only of small floes, we were led to hope that the strong east winds would soon disperse them. But the very contrary really happened, for the low temperatures, the calms, and falls of snow bound the floes of ice only the more closely together, and within a few days congealed them into one single field, in the midst of which the ship remained fast and immoveable. Our surroundings were monotonous beyond description,—one vast unattractive white

surface, and even the high-lands of Novaya Zemlya, were covered with freshly fallen snow.

2. To reach the coast of Siberia under these circumstances had become an impossibility, and even in the event of our being liberated, the search for a winter harbour in Novaya Zemlya would be a matter of peril and difficulty. Yet we calculated confidently on this contingency and employed our enforced inactivity in completing our preparations for sledge journeys during the autumn, although we could not but feel, that their importance must be of secondary interest and value in a country so well known as Novaya Zemlya. Meantime we drifted slowly along the coast in a northerly direction and apparently under the influence of a current, which has been often observed on the northern coasts of Novaya Zemlya. But the gloom of our situation, as we became conscious of our captivity, was more distinctly and painfully felt. On the 1st of September the temperature sank nine degrees below zero ($-9°$ R.), and the few and limited spaces of open water round our floe disappeared. The sun now remained six hours below the horizon, and the formation of young ice in a single night often reached such a thickness, that we soon perceived that our last hope for this year lay in the setting in of heavy equinoctial storms to break up the ice-fields.

3. On the 2nd of September a fissure running through our floe reached the after-part of the *Tegetthoff* and opened into a "lead," and even our floe partially broke up; but this availed us nothing, for the ship itself remained fast on a huge fragment. During the night of Sept. 3, the after-part of the *Tegetthoff* was gently raised for the first time by the pressure and driving from

ATTEMPTS TO GET FREE IN SEPTEMBER.

beneath of the ice; yet of the formidable nature of such pressure we had as yet no presentiment. Though our situation seemed desperate, it was not attended by immediate danger, and, condemned as we were to inactivity, we found the amusement and occupation we needed in skating on the young ice, which covered many of the newly formed ice-holes, between the ice-floes. Besides the duty of making and recording meteorological observations, the training of the dogs, the bringing ice to the kitchen to be transformed into water, the manufacture of oil, expeditions on foot to explore the country, were the only forms in which our energies could be exerted. Absolute loneliness surrounded us; even the Arctic sea-gull (*Larus glaucus*) and the gray stormy petrel (*Procellaria glacialis L.*) of the polar region were but rarely seen, and a bear, which, Sept. 5, came within forty paces of the ship, was driven away by the awkwardness of our hunters. The cold became more and more intense and the weather more gloomy. Sept. 2, the cabin lamp had to be lit for the first time about half-past nine o'clock, and on the 3rd we began to heat the interior parts of the ship, the temperature of which had been for some time at zero; and on the 11th, the first fiery belts of the Aurora flamed in the northern heavens. On the 9th and 10th, there was a very heavy storm from the north-east, which drove us back for a short time towards the west, and partially broke up our floe, but all the efforts of the next week to destroy the connection of what remained by sawing and blasting proved unsuccessful. Blasting with powder, whether above or below the surface-ice, proved ineffectual. Even old fissures in the ice appeared to defy further disruption, segments which had been laboriously made by sawing, froze again almost immediately, and even the application of steam was powerless to set our floe in motion and force the breaking-up of the parts which had been sawn through. It was of no avail that, up to Oct. 7, we kept open a trench round the ship, by destroying in the day the ice which had been

SEAL-HUNTING —SEPTEMBER 1872.

formed during the night : the expected disruption of our ice-field never happened. Dark streaks in the heavens still proclaimed, that we were in the neighbourhood of open water, and though they seemed only to indicate "leads" of no great breadth or extent, they helped to sustain our hopes. But these were soon doomed to be disappointed, for even these "leads" closed up, and *at the same time the temperature fell to an unusually low degree.* On the 15th of September, we had 15 degrees of cold, and on the 19th the temperature fell 18·6 degrees below zero (C.). To add to this, there were frequent falls of drifting snow. As long as fissures remained, we had opportunities of seal-hunting, but by the end of the month the "ice-holes" were overspread with spongy ice, which hindered the movements of our boats within them. The alternate openings and closings of the waterways around us seemed in our monotonous life a harmless spectacle, for the lofty walls of piled-up ice had not as yet for us the language of imminent and threatening dangers.

4. Sept. 22, there was a fissure in the ice about thirty paces from the ship, and we quickly put on board all the materials which were lying on the floe, believing that the moment of our deliverance had come. But no such moment came, nor did the equinoctial storms which we expected set in ; *we continued to drift still further to the north;* and on Oct. 2, we had passed the seventy-seventh degree of north latitude. In the beginning of this month a storm, which lasted but a short time, opened up a large "ice-hole" near the after-part of the ship, and forthwith we set to work to open a passage through our floe in order to reach it, but two days afterwards this "ice-hole" also closed up. Yet amid all our

mishaps we forgot not on the 4th of October—the name-day of his Majesty the Emperor Francis Joseph I.—the homage which was due to our noble and gracious Sovereign. The ship was gaily dressed with flags, and a rifle-match, in which watches and pipes were

SHOOTING AT A TARGET, OCTOBER 1872.

the prizes, scared away for a short afternoon the sad impressions of the moment.

5. Encounters with polar bears afforded us much excitement. On the 6th of October, our first bear was killed and divided among the dogs, for as yet we had not learnt to regard the flesh of these animals as the most

precious part of our provisions. A fox also, the first seen during this expedition, showed himself during the previous night. He had evidently come from Novaya Zemlya, and his curiosity had led him close to the ship, from whence he was driven by the dogs. It now became indispensable for everyone who left the immediate neighbourhood of the ship to carry arms with him, and the neglect of this precaution had sometimes rather ludicrous, at other times somewhat serious consequences. On the 11th of October I left the ship unarmed and with no other companion than our Lapland dog, Pekel, to employ myself in the harmless occupation of piling up a tower of ice. Working as I was in a stooping position, I was unconscious of what was immediately around me, when on a sudden the loud barking of Pekel caused me to raise myself, and I saw a bear quite close before me. Shaking his head and making a snuffling noise, he came on towards me. In the expectation that some of the people engaged on deck would see my critical position, I contented myself with shaking my fist at him, unwilling to reveal any weakness to my enemy. As this, however, seemed to produce no effect, I cried out repeatedly, "A bear!" At last I saw Klotz, who was on deck, go to the stand of arms, but with such stoical composure, that I ceased to trust to others, and left to the bear, who had now advanced to a distance of about fifteen paces from me, the glory of forcing his enemy to take to flight.

6. In the first days of October the temperature rose considerably, the thermometer standing a little below zero (R.). This was due to south-west winds, and to the temporary extension of the "ice-holes" in our immediate neighbourhood. The days now became shorter, the sun surrounded with red masses of clouds set behind barriers of blackish-blue ice, and an ever-deepening twilight, followed his disappearance. Sept. 29, a "snowfinch" flew from the coast of Novaya Zemlya to the ship, hopped about the deck for a little time, and after delighting us all by his little song, again left us. Some few sea-gulls still wended their flight to the spaces of water in our neighbourhood. Skimming over the top of the mast, they seemed to gaze down upon us, and then with a shrill cry darted away like arrows towards the south. There was something melancholy in this departure of the birds; it seemed as if all creatures were retiring from the long reign of night which was before us. In order to divert our attention from the dreadful monotony of our captivity by some occupation in the open air, we fell on the plan of building houses of ice round the ship. The activity of a building-yard reigned on our ice-floe; heavy ice-tables were broken or sawed through, the dogs in the sledges carried the

fragments to their appointed places, and with these blocks we raised crystal walls and towers. Snow, mixed with sea-water, furnished an inexhaustible source of the most excellent mortar ; and while we worked laboriously at these meaningless erections, we earned at least by our labour the reward of sleep free from care.

PARHELIA ON THE COAST OF NOVAYA ZEMLYA.

7. As we drifted helplessly northward, the coasts of Novaya Zemlya receded gradually from our gaze. Hitherto we had lain close to the land, which with its rounded mountains and valleys filled with glaciers seemed a miniature of Alpine scenery. Daily almost the gigantic luminous arcs of parhelia stood above it, the usual precursors of stormy weather or heavy falls

of snow. Towards the north and north-east the country becomes flatter, and runs into glacier-wastes little raised above the level of the sea. The topography of the northern parts of Novaya Zemlya is complete confusion. The only survey which exists—that of Lütke—extends no further than Cape Nassau. The maps of the Barentz Isles are frequently in contradiction with fact, and their correction is extremely desirable. Though this land was of no value for our object, yet it was still land, and it seemed also to us, drifting as we did, the symbol of the stable and immovable. But now it was gradually disappearing from our eyes. During September we had moved slowly, but with October we drifted at a greater rate, so that by the 12th of this month we saw nothing but a line of heights some thirty miles off, towards the south. At last every trace of land disappeared from our gaze; a hopeless waste received us, in which no man could tell how long we should be, nor how far we should penetrate.

CHAPTER IV.

THE "TEGETTHOFF" FAST BESET IN THE ICE.

1. AUTUMN was passing away, the days were getting shorter and in our immediate neighbourhood no movement in the ice was perceptible, save that we had drifted continuously towards the north-east; sometimes, though rarely, a fissure in the ice grew to the proportions of an "ice hole," only, however, to be quickly frozen over and present a surface for our skates. There lay the frozen sea, the picture of dull hopeless monotony; shelter there was none. Our floe, though it seemed to combine the conveniences of a winter harbour, could not stand the test of closer observation, the illusion of such a notion must be short-lived. But many signs now indicated the insecurity of our position. Fields of ice in our neighbourhood cracked and split asunder, and piled up masses floated round us, silent preachers, as it were, of the destruction which ice pressure could produce.

2. A change, however, was soon to come over the scene.

On the evening of October 12 we imagined that the cabin lamp oscillated, and consequently that our floe was in motion. On the same night we were conscious of a violent movement in the ice. A dreadful day was the 13th of October,—a Sunday; it was decisive of the fate of the expedition. To the superstitious amongst us the number 13 was clothed with a profound significance: the committee of the expedition had been constituted on February 13; on the 13th of January the keel of the *Tegetthoff* had been laid down; on the 13th of April she was launched; on the 13th of June we left Bremerhaven; on the 13th of July, Tromsoe; after a voyage of 13 days we had arrived at the ice, and on the 13th October the temperature marked 13 degrees below zero. In the morning of that day, as we sat at breakfast, our floe burst across immediately under the ship. Rushing on deck we discovered that we were surrounded and squeezed by the ice; the after part of the ship was already nipped and pressed, and the rudder, which was the first to encounter its assault, shook and groaned; but as its great weight did not admit of its being shipped, we were content to lash it firmly. We next sprang on the ice, the tossing tremulous motion of which literally filled the air with noises as of shrieks and howls, and we quickly got on board all the materials which were lying on the floe, and bound the fissures of the ice hastily together by ice-anchors and cables, filling them up with snow, in the hope that frost would complete our work, though we felt that a single heave might shatter our labours. But, just as in the risings of a people, the wave of revolt spreads on every side, so now the ice uprose against us. Mountains threateningly reared themselves from out the level fields of ice and the low groan which issued from its depths grew into a deep rumbling sound, and at last rose into a furious howl as of myriads of voices. Noise and confusion reigned supreme, and step by step destruction drew nigh in the crashing together of the fields of ice. Our floe was now crushed, and its blocks piled up into mountains, drove hither and thither. Here, they towered fathoms high above the ship, and forced the protecting timbers of massive oak, as if in mockery of their purpose, against the hull of the vessel; there masses of ice fell down as into an abyss under the ship, to be engulfed in the rushing waters, so that the quantity of ice beneath the ship was continually increased, and at last it began to raise her quite above the level of the sea. About 11.30 in the forenoon according to our usual custom, a portion of the Bible was read on deck, and this day, quite accidentally, the portion read was the history of Joshua: but if in his day the sun stood still, it was more than the ice now showed any inclination to do.

3. The terrible commotion going on around us prevented us from seeing anything distinctly. The sky too was overcast, the sun's place could only be conjectured. In all haste we began to make ready to abandon the ship, in case it should be crushed, a fate which seemed inevitable, if she were not sufficiently raised through the pressure of the ice. About 12.30 the pressure reached a frightful height, every part of the vessel strained and groaned; the crew, who had been sent down to dine, rushed on deck. The *Tegetthoff* had heeled over on her side, and huge piles of ice threatened to precipitate themselves upon her. But the pressure abated, and the ship righted herself; and about one o'clock, when the danger was in some degree over, the crew went below to dine. But again a strain was felt through the vessel, everything which hung freely began to oscillate violently, and all hastened on deck, some with the unfinished dinner in their hands, others stuffing it into their pockets. Calmly and silently amid the loud sounds emitted by the ice in its violent movement, the officers assumed and carried out the special duty which had been assigned to each in the contemplated abandonment of the ship. Lieutenant Weyprecht got ready the boats, Brosch and Orel cleared out the supply of provision to be taken in them, Kepes, our doctor, had an eye to his drugs, the Tyrolese opened the magazine, and got out the rifles and ammunition I myself attended

to the sledges, the tents, and the sacks for sleeping in and distributed to the crew their fur coats. We now stood ready to start, each with a bundle—whither, no one pretended to know! For not a fragment of the ice around us had remained whole; nowhere could the eye discover a still perfect and uninjured floe, to serve as a place of refuge, as a vast floe had before been to the crew of the *Hansa*. Nay, not a block, not a table of ice was at rest, all shapes and sizes of it were in active motion, some rearing up, some turning and twisting, none on the level. A sledge would at once have been swallowed up, and in this very circumstance lay the horror of our situation. For, if the ship should sink, whither should we go, even with the smallest stock of provisions?—amid this confusion, how reach the land 30 miles distant without the most indispensable necessaries?

4. The dogs, too, demanded our attention. They had sprung on chests and stared on the waves of ice, as they rose and roared. Every trace of his fox-nature had disappeared from "Sumbu." His look, at other times so full of cunning, had assumed an expression of timidity and humility, and, unbidden, he offered his paw to all passers by. The Lapland dog, little Pekel, sprang upon me, licked my hand, and looked out on the ice as if he meant to ask me what all this meant. The large

Newfoundlands stood motionless, like scared chamois, on the piles of chests.

5. About 4 p.m. the pressure moderated; an hour afterwards there was a calm, and with more composure we could now survey our position. The carpenter shovelled away the snow from the deck in order to inspect the seams. They were still uninjured. The knees and cross-beams still held, and no very great quantity of water was found in the hold. This result we owed solely to the strength of our ship and to her fine lines, which enabled her to rise when nipped and pressed, while her interior, so well laden as to become a solid body, increased her powers of resistance. Everything was again restored to its place, so that it was possible to go up and down the cabin stairs without great difficulty, and in the evening the water in the hold, which had risen 13 inches, was pumped out to its normal depth of 6 inches. We went down into the cabin to rest, but though thankful and joyful for the issue, our minds, were clouded with care and anxiety. Henceforth we regarded every noise with suspicious apprehensions, like a population which lives within an area of earthquakes. The long winter nights and their fearful cold were before us; we were drifting into unknown regions, utterly uncertain of the end. When night came, we fell asleep with our clothes on,

though our sleep was disturbed every now and then by the onsets of the ice, recurring less frequently and in diminished force; but daily—and for *one hundred and thirty days*—we went through the same experiences in greater or lesser measure, almost always in sunless darkness. It was, however, a fortunate circumstance for us that we encountered the first assaults of the ice at a time when we were still able to see; for instead of the calm preparations we were able to make, hurry and confusion would have been inevitable had these assaults surprised us amid the Polar darkness.

6. Early in the morning of Oct. 14 we all met at breakfast, but on every face there lay an expression of grave thoughtfulness, for each of us was contemplating the long perspective of those dreary nights, in which we should drift without a goal in the awful wastes of the Frozen Sea. The speedy restoration of our floe was now our most earnest desire. It was only severe frost and heavy falls of snow—as we vainly imagined—which could cement the chaos of broken fragments around us and form from them a new floe; for as yet we had not learnt by experience, that severe cold in itself, unaccompanied with wind, is sufficient to break up the fields of ice, from the contraction which it causes. We deluded ourselves with another consolation —we imagined that the ice-pressures would cease, as

AN OCTOBER NIGHT IN THE ICE.

soon as we passed the eastern extremity of Novaya Zemlya, and that in the Sea of Kara we should drift without encountering the pressures, due as we conceived, to our nearness to land. But vain also was this hope, for we were drifting not into the Sea of Kara but towards the north-east. We should have found, even in that sea, that pressures from the ice may occur within the Frozen Ocean, however, as well as at its coasts. The masses of ice which caused our disasters probably came from that sea.

7. The time subsequent to this crisis was full of painful and anxious moments, but a chronological description of the events of each day, involving a mere repetition of our sad impressions, would be wearisome to the reader. I will, therefore, transfer from my journal such portions of it as most forcibly express the thoughts that passed through the minds of the handful of men on board the *Tegetthoff* during those terrible days:—

"*October* 14.—About half-past eight o'clock in the evening a new fissure in the ice appeared astern of the ship; a strain was felt throughout her timbers; in a moment every one in his fur dress and with his bundle in his hand was on deck: so will it be, perhaps, throughout the winter—what a life!

"*October* 15.—All had slept in their clothes. Fresh

pressures from the ice were felt about eight o'clock in the morning, not so powerful as on the 13th, but of such force that all sprang from their berths and within a minute again stood ready on the deck. Much ice had been forced under the afterpart of the ship, which was raised up by the pressure. When all was calm every one set to work to make a bag to contain the gear he meant to take, if the ship should be crushed. Mine contained the following articles: one pair of fur gloves, one pair of woollen gloves, a pair of snow spectacles, six pencils, a rubber, three note-books, the journal of my Greenland expedition, a book of drawings, ten ball cartridges, two pairs of stockings, a knife, a case of needles and thread. On the 13th we had neglected to provide ourselves with maps of Novaya Zemlya; two of these I now included among my stock of necessaries. Six Lefaucheur rifles, four Werndl-rifles, two thousand cartridges, two large and two smaller sledges, a tent for ten, one for six men, two great sleeping sacks, each for eight, and a smaller one for six men, were placed in the boats. Although all these preparations would have been quite vain if the ship had sunk with the ice in motion to crush us, we must, for our mutual encouragement, keep up the appearance of believing in them. About six o'clock in the evening the full moon rose, like a copper coin fresh from the mint, above our horizon on the deep blue of the heavens. In the evening the ice was at rest, and for the first time for some days we ventured to undress on going to bed.

"*October* 16.—Slept without care or disturbance till two o'clock in the morning, when pressure from the ice again set in, and all rushed on deck. Some of the crew threw out on the ice the antlers of a rein-deer of Novaya Zemlya,—for according to a superstition of the seamen the horns of a rein-deer are the generators of mischief! The ice again calm, and I fell asleep from exhaustion; but about half-past five in the morning there was a new pressure of about twenty minutes' duration, and almost as fearful as on the 13th of the month. The exceeding haste with which every one rushes up from below, as soon as the ship begins to strain, shows the effect which the noise makes on us; it is impossible to become accustomed to it; every one runs on deck. Again the ice rests, but about half-past seven in the morning, another pressure, which almost tore away the beams protecting the hull and the davits to which they were fastened. The ship, however, rights herself. To-day the ice which overhung our bulwarks was dug away to prevent masses of it falling on the deck. In the evening, diminished pressure from the ice; at night, glorious moonlight scenery; nothing more peaceful, but nothing more illusive, than such a scene at such an hour.

"*October* 17.—All quiet during the night till Lusina came to announce with a voice as from the grave, that the ship was making more water, sixteen inches in the forepart, eleven inches amidships. East wind, with heavy drifting snowstorms—during the day once only a strain of short duration was felt in the ship, as a new fissure opened in the piled-up ice on our starboard quarter.

"*October* 18.—Our anxieties somewhat abate and our watchful state of preparation to leave the ship relaxes, and most of us determine once more to undress for the night. After several weeks the sun, which had been obscured by the weather, becomes visible, rising 2° 25' above the horizon; the temperature stands at $-23°$ (R.), and our latitude is 77° 48'.

"*October* 19.—Straining in the ship; the sun rose about a quarter past eight, but was soon veiled in frosty vapours.

"*October* 20.—The hull of the ship is still without its necessary protection of ice and snow, while we are wrapt in furs and wear rein-deer shoes and felt-boots. In the evening a faint mock moon was visible.

"*October* 21.—At night we were alarmed by a loud sound, and in a few minutes all were on deck with their fur clothes on—a fissure had opened on the starboard side of the ship connecting itself with that which had

THE MOON WITH ITS HALO

been formed astern of the ship. In an hour this fissure had widened about four feet, and we worked for some hours by the light of lamps to fill it up with snow and pieces of ice. The low temperature ($-23\frac{1}{2}°$ R.) led us to expect that this chasm would be bridged over without further effort on our part. The moon stood surrounded by a vast halo in the heavens and illuminated the awful loneliness of our abode. Once more a calm! When any one comes down from the deck into the cabin, the eyes of all are involuntarily turned upon him to read in the expression of his face what is going on above, and each dreads to hear it said, that the ice is in motion. In the afternoon, when the fissure closed, we heard the old dull sound from the ice, and the ship strained violently, and all were on deck ready to leave. About nine o'clock in the evening the motion of the ice was again felt. Uncertain and full of fears as to what the night might bring forth, we go early to rest; no one knows how short that rest may be. Even Klotz lays aside his stoical calmness, and the philosophical dignity of his remarks departs, when his comrades spring from their berths and rush on deck with their bundles. The frozen pumps are daily thawed by boiling water; to-day the shaft of one of them broke, through the excessive strain put upon it.

October 22.—During the, night motion in the ice. At 9.30 A.M. the sun rose, and attains its meridian altitude at 1° 41'. In the evening the fissure in the ice again opens. Rents and small "ice-holes" are all round us, and frosty vapour fills the air. To-day the skull of a bear was thrown out on the ice, the crew asserting that mischief comes from the possession of it!

October 23.—During the night violent movement in the ice; the sound produced resembles the noise of a fleet of paddle-wheel steamships, steaming now with full, now with half power. The height of the sun to-day above the horizon was a little above one degree, its form was distorted by refraction into an egg-like shape, and its edges were in constant vibration.

October 24.—The daylight is now so feeble that the lamps have to be lighted during the day, with the exception of two or three hours in the forenoon. Many of the crew are suffering from frost-bites on their hands, in consequence of their exposure in removing the unnecessary rigging, and in the preparations to facilitate the removal of our stock of provisions, in the event of our being forced to abandon the vessel.

October 25.—In the afternoon we made an attempt to drive the dog sledges, but the snow, in spite of the low temperature, lay in such masses between the small hummocks and on the few level places, that they sank deep into it. It is storms of wind only that harden the snow, and for some time we have had calms or light breezes. In the evening there was a movement in the ice astern of the ship, accompanied with the highest soprano tones. The noise the ice makes in its pressure very much resembles the piping and howling of a storm among rocky cliffs or through the rigging

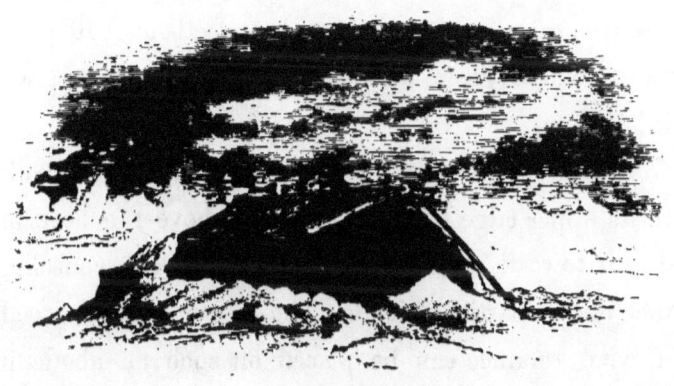

OUR COAL HOUSE ON THE FLOE.

of a ship. About half-past ten at night, the oscillating movements of the ice, occurring at definite intervals, made it appear as if they arose from a swell of the ocean. The ship groans and creaks constantly; indeed, creaking and groaning are weak expressions for such a noise. Once more all are ready. We begin to fear that the ice will never rest.

October 26.—Pressure throughout the whole night.

Armed and provided with lanterns, we used the sledges to remove two boats, 150 logs of wood, fifty planks, and a supply of coals, to the port side of the vessel, and chose a stronger floe, on which to build a house of refuge. Tired and exhausted, we fell asleep in spite of the straining and creaking of the vessel.

October 27.—The sun at noon was scarcely visible above the horizon. At night of the same day a strong wind from the south-east opened a fissure on the starboard side of the vessel and about 150 paces from it, which grew into the dimensions of an "ice-hole."

October 28.—To-day the sun took leave of us. Only with its upper edge had it appeared above the horizon, and sent towards us its mild beams like the consoling glance of a departing friend. The coal-house is finished. But what reliance can be placed on such an abode in such a position? A storm may carry away the planks which form its roof; sparks from a fire may set fire to its walls and consume it; and at any moment, through a pressure opening up an abyss beneath, it may sink and be engulfed. Two o'clock in the afternoon, the groaning sound comes from the piles of ice around us; our floe appears to twist somewhat, and the pressure of the ice will probably soon begin.

October 29.—During the night a noise in the ice,

which, though it did not further disturb us, was yet witness enough that it is ever ready to disturb us. The sun no longer appears; only a rosy light at noon in the heavens.

October 30.—At half-past three o'clock in the morning there was a dreadful straining and creaking in the ship: at once we sprang out of our berths, and stood on deck with our fur garments on and with our bags as before. New fissures had appeared which rapidly enlarge themselves; the two boats and the coal-house are now surrounded by up-forced masses of ice and separated from us. Then a pause! There is however no real repose, and the least sound on deck, the falling of anything heavy—at other times quite unnoticed—alarms us into the expectation of new onsets. At noon, as we sat at dinner, there was renewed and excessive straining in the ship, and even in the cabin we heard such a rushing sound in the ice without, that it seemed as if the whole frozen sea would the next moment boil and rise in vapour. During all the afternoon the noise continues, and all the fissures send forth dense vapours, like hot springs. During the day no quiet for reading or working, and every night almost our sleep is disturbed by a horrible awaking within a great creaking, groaning coffin. Men can accustom themselves to almost anything; but to these daily recurring shocks, and the constantly renewed question as to the end and issue of it all, we cannot grow accustomed."

8. There is however such an intolerable monotony in my diary, that, to spare my readers, I thus, in a few words, resuming its contents, describe our situation:—
"One of us, to-day, remarked very truly, that he saw perfectly well how one might lose his reason with the continuance of these sudden and incessant assaults. It is not dangers that we fear, but worse far; we are kept in a constant state of readiness to meet destruction, and know not whether it will come to-day, or to-morrow, or in a year. Every night we are startled out of sleep, and, like hunted animals, up we spring to await amid an awful darkness the end of an enterprise from which all hope of success has departed. It becomes at last a mere mechanical process to seize our rifles and our bag of necessaries and rush on deck. In the daytime, leaning over the bulwarks of the ship, which trembles, yea, almost quivers the while, we look out on a continual work of destruction going on, and at night as we listen to the loud and ever-increasing noises of the ice, we gather that the forces of our enemy are increasing."

CHAPTER V.

OUR FIRST WINTER (1872) *IN THE ICE.*

1. In the beginning of November we were already environed by a deep twilight; but our dreary waste had become of magical beauty; the rigging, white with frost, stood out, spectre-like, against the grey-blue of the heavens; the ice, broken into a thousand forms and overspread with a covering of snow, had now assumed the cold pure aspect of alabaster shaded with the tender hues of arragonite. Southward at noon we saw veils of frosty vapour rise into the carmine-coloured sky out of the fissures and "ice-holes," in which the water seemed to boil.

2. All our preparations for wintering had now been completed. Lieutenant Weyprecht struck the top-masts to diminish pressure from the wind: some sails were still kept set, in order that the ship, in the event of her being set free, might at once get under weigh. The fore part of the ship only could be covered in as a tent, for the preparations to abandon her in case of need

compelled us to leave her after part uncovered. There, in perfect order, lay all the materials we meant to take with us, our provisions, ammunition, tents, sledges, &c. The ship was surrounded with a wall of snow and ice, which

THE TWILIGHT IN NOVEMBER, 1872.

we constantly restored, whenever it was injured by pressure from without, and her deck was gradually overspread with a mantle of snow, which contributed however, to maintain an equable warmth in the ship. Our distance from land rendered it impossible to cover the deck with a layer of sand, which would have prevented the melting of the snow from the warmth of the ship.

3. The temperature of November rose once only—about the middle of the month—considerably; but, except on that occasion, the thermometer stood with tolerable regularity below $-20°$ R., and on the 20th of the month it reached its minimum at $-29°$ R. Winds, from whatever quarter they might blow, constantly raised the temperature, because the colder air was thus modified by the warmer which lay above the open spaces of sea-water: calms were accompanied by a rapid intensification of cold. Wind, increased drifting, pressure, and the formation of fissures—all these are naturally connected. New openings were quickly covered with young ice, which presented a smooth surface when formed by less intense cold, but when the temperature fell lower, its saline contents were exuded in a moist, tough layer, which lay on its surface about an inch thick. In this state of the ice, sledge-travelling was rendered more difficult, and even walking was far from easy; for it is only under a temperature ranging from $-16°$ to $-20°$ that this layer is frozen. The incessant rending of the ice-sheet, by exposing the warmer surface of the sea, tends to mitigate the cold, while, on the other hand, the freezing of these fissures augments the quantity of ice.

4. In the beginning of the month our nights were dark.

and it was only occasionally that the light of the aurora and meteors visited us with their fleeting splendours. Although in clear weather day was still distinguishable from night, yet the darkness, even at noon, was so great, that mists could not be seen, but felt only, and it was

SUMBU CHASED FOR A FOX.

no longer possible, without the light of a lantern, to make even the slightest sketch, or to take aim with the rifle. Hence, when we met with bears we could not be certain of our aim, if they were at any distance from us, and, on one occasion, Sumbu was mistaken for a fox, chased, and but for my coming up would have been shot.

5. The first days of November passed away without any new disturbance from the movement of the masses of ice, and our feeling of security grew apace, and with it our hopes revived, never again to leave us entirely, not even when the pressures returned, as they did too soon. Once more the fields of ice, firmly pressed together, were rent asunder; fissures opened out, and shone in the moonlight like rivers of silver. The night of Nov. 20 was one of extreme anxiety. A mountain formed of piles of broken ice bore down on us amid a fearful din threatening to bury the ship. Silent, and conscious of our utter helplessness, we watched this gigantic heap of crashing ice-tables, drifting nearer and nearer, crushing as it advanced the heaviest pieces of ice with a noise which echoed through our ship. Escape seemed impossible: and Providence alone arrested its career. This night the crew received each an extra glass of grog to obliterate the impression of this terrible crisis.

6. With the exception of books, we had no other amusement than short expeditions, never extending beyond a mile from the ship, in which we were accompanied by all the dogs. We generally set out with two small sledges, and when the moon was not shining, with our rifles ready to fire, for the darkness and the utter absence of open spaces on the ice imposed the utmost caution against bears. At a very short distance we

could see nothing of the ship, and only by our footsteps on the snow could we make out where we were and find the way back. In these expeditions we were exposed to another danger—the risk of being cut off from the ship by the breaking-up of one of the drifting floes. Even the dogs felt the insecurity of recently-formed ice, and put their feet on it with fear and hesitation, and only by compulsion. There seemed to be a cunning agreement among them to shirk the work altogether; for they often rushed away into the coal-house, and threw the harness of the sledges into inextricable confusion.

7. December came, but it brought no change in our situation. Our life became more and more monotonous; one day differed in no respect from another, it was but a mere succession of dates, and time was reckoned merely by the hours for eating and sleeping. The ice, however, did not share in the universal repose. It was never weary of threatening; no day elapsed without movement on its part. My journal records December 1, 8, 9, 19, 20, 21, 24, 26, 28, 29, 30 and 31, as days of special disturbance and agitation. On the 20th, as we were talking in the coal-house of the approaching festival of Christmas, a sudden violent movement of the ice surprised us, and rushing out we found that the floe on which the house stood was breaking up. With all haste we endeavoured to save as much as possible of the coal

and materials, and moved them close to the ship. The minimum temperature of December was $-26°$ R.; the mean of the whole month amounted to $-24°$ R.; and the extreme of cold, $-29°$ R., was reached on the 26th. A few days before Christmas the temperature rose to a little below $-20°$ R. It may be observed that the lower temperatures were registered during the prevalence of winds from the south-east, and the higher during winds from the north.

8. When the moon returned in the middle of December, our sledge expeditions were extended to a distance of $1\frac{1}{2}$ miles from the ship, over snow and hummocks, to recently frozen ice-holes, the lonely beauty of which, edged with dark masses of ice, in the distance, and lying under the clear silver light of the moon, filled us with feelings of profound melancholy. On returning from one of these expeditions to our vessel, after we had unharnessed the dogs we heard loud barks from Sumbu, and looking round saw a bear close beside him, which Orel managed to shoot dead when he was not above five paces from the rope-ladder on the port side of the vessel. He was at once cut up, the dogs meanwhile looking on with profound attention; and in reward for his watchfulness, Sumbu was indulged with an extra good feast—the heart and tongue of the bear, which, as yet, we ourselves had not learnt to eat

and enjoy. On the 18th, however, he encountered our heavy displeasure for the offence of frightening off a fox, which had ventured to come very near the vessel.

9. When there was no moon it was perfectly dark, even during the day; but on December 14, in a very clear

ENCOUNTER WITH A POLAR BEAR.

forenoon, we saw in the south a tender orange segment of light, three or four degrees above the horizon, edged with green, sharply defined against the dark sky, and when the moon, high in the heavens, faced this arch of light, a peculiar faint twilight was observable. But generally there was no difference between the light of

midday and the light of midnight. The heavens were usually overcast, and the light of the aurora, during the few minutes of its greatest intensity, seldom exceeded that of the moon in its first quarter. But how deep would be the night of the Polar regions, if the land, instead of being white with snow, were covered with forests! On December 20 we were unable, even at noon, to read anything but the titles of books of the largest type; a man's eyes were invisible at the distance of a few paces, and at fifty even the stoutest ropes of the ship were scarcely discernible. The effect of the long Polar night —when the range of the light of a lamp is the whole world for man—is most oppressive to the feelings; nor can habit ever reconcile those who have lived under the influences of civilization to its gloom and solitude. It can be a home only to men who spend their existence in eating and drinking and sleeping, without any disturbing recollection of a better existence. The depression was made more intense by the consciousness that we had been driven into an utterly unknown region and with our eyes bound. Work, incessant work, was the only resource in these circumstances.

10. Again from my journal I reproduce some passages which express the feelings which passed through our minds—through mine at least—during this season of the *Tegetthoff's* first winter in the ice:—"*December*

21.—The middle of the long night. It is noon, and, though nothing can be lighter than the colour of all that surrounds us—of the snow—yet it is as dark as midnight. Nothing but a pale yellow sheen hovers over the south. The sun has sunk below the horizon 11° 40′ and we should have to ascend a mountain eighteen and a half (German) miles high in order to behold it. Nothing is to be seen, neither bears nor men, and we only hear the steps of those who are near us. We see but the confused outline even of the ship, as she drifts hither and thither with the floe, a prisoner in the fetters of the ice, the sport of winds and currents, carrying her further and further into the still and silent realm of death. A definite object, with hope to inspire them, raises men above toils and troubles of every kind; but exile like ours, when the sacrifice seems useless, is hard to be borne. An inexorable 'No' lays its ban on every hope, and daily struggle for self-preservation is our lot. If we attempt to fathom destiny, our utmost hopes are liberation from our icy captivity some time next summer, and the reaching the coast of Siberia. Siberia a hope! And yet how changeable are the feelings when the reign of monotony is interrupted! The moon is up—darkness exists no more. In the North the moon is an event—it is life, everything almost; it is the only link which connects us with the far distant home. As its beams fall on the meanest forms, diamonds blaze forth in its light from the snow and the frost, and the soul feels the beauty of the transformation. She looks down on us like a returning friend that watches over us, and unfolds bewitching forms and magic images to cheer us. Two weeks ago she rose above the horizon, first as a blood-red disk, then paled as she climbed higher and higher, till she stands out the clear, silver-bright, full moon."

11. Christmas had come; the season when in the forests of our far distant home the branches of the pine trees are heavy laden with snow, and which ever comes back with the memories of the days of our youth, and with the remembrances of our families and absent friends. Only for a short time, about noon, we were made uneasy by a movement and pressure of the ice. But the alarm passed away, and we gathered together for a choice and gorgeous feast both on Christmas Eve and Christmas Day, and each of the cabin-mess had a bottle of good wine to himself. Carlsen and Lusina were our guests. Each of the crew received half a bottle of wine, together with a quarter of a bottle of "artificial wine,"[1] and in addition an allowance of grog, so weak, however, that even a baby might have drunk it without harm. Dried fish, roast bear, well kept and seasoned, nuts and the like

[1] A decoction prepared by Kepes.

contributed in their way to heighten the joyous feelings, which, this day at least, animate even the most miserable of men. The dogs, at other times so insatiable, had for once enough and to spare, and carried off the fragments to bury them in the snow. The contents of a chest full of presents, which we had brought with us, were distributed by lot, and great was the delight of those who won a bottle of rum or a few cigars.

12. The last day of the year 1872 afforded us no very happy thoughts as we looked back on its events; it had been to us a year of disappointments. The comparison drawn between our actual condition and the expectations we had so ardently cherished seemed full of the bitterest irony. This day also, about noon, a pressure from the ice, which lasted but a short time, alarmed us all, and we rushed on deck to make our usual preparations. The enemy, however, passed away without further disturbance, and cheerfully and socially we awaited the first hour of the new year. With a bottle of champagne, one of the two still left, we meant to greet its coming in, with that hopefulness of mind, which seems inextinguishable in all the changes and chances of life. But the champagne, alas! proved a delusion. Klotz, the Tyrolese, in one of his brown studies exposed this precious bottle for four hours to a temperature of $-23°$ R., and when he produced it, the bottle had burst and

the wine was thoroughly frozen. At midnight the crew serenaded us, and we afterwards marched forth in a body with torches and walked round the ship, whose rigging glowed in the light of the tarred torches. The frosted fur garments of the men seemed edged with shining light, and a red glare fell on the masses of ice.

13. To-day, too, we allowed the dogs to descend into our cabin,—the constant object of their longings. The poor animals were so dazzled by looking at our lamp, that they almost took it for the sun itself; but by and by their attention was directed exclusively to the rich remains of our dinner, the sight of which appeared completely to satisfy their notions of the wonders of the cabin. After behaving themselves with great propriety, they again quietly withdrew, all except Jubinal, who appeared to be indignant at the deceitfulness of our conduct, inasmuch as we had allowed him to starve so long on dried horse-flesh and on crushed bear's head, while we revelled in luxury. He accordingly made his way into Lieutenant Brosch's cabin, where, discovering a mountain of macaroni, he immediately attacked it, and warned us off from every attempt to rescue it, by growling fiercely till he had finished it all. Sumbu, however, with much levity, suffered himself to be made drunk by the sailors with rum, and everything which he had scraped together for weeks and buried in the snow and

so carefully watched, was stolen from him by the other dogs in one night.

14. Another year had now glided away. Looking anxiously into the future, we shortsighted mortals saw the fulfilment of our highest wishes in being liberated

CARLSEN MAKES THE ENTRY IN THE LOG.

from the floe. In the pious manner of the whalers of the Arctic Ocean, Carlsen wrote this day in the log : " Önsker at Gud maa vere med os i det nye aar, da kan intet vare imod os."—*May God be with us in the new year and nothing can be against us.*" In this new year, with its happier issues, was verified again the eternal truth, that Providence acts in ways not to be fathomed, and that it is folly in man to mark out his own path beforehand according to his own mind. The sun of this new year, whose beams were to light us to new lands and discoveries, was still low beneath the horizon.

CHAPTER VI.

LIFE ON BOARD THE "TEGETTHOFF."

1. LIKE a spectre in white, the ship stretches out her arms, as if in silent complaint, towards the heaven, and rests, in cruel mockery of her destiny, on a mountain, not of water, but of ice, and seems like a building ready to fall in. A wall of snow and ice surrounds her hull, snow lies thick on her deck, and her rigging is stiffened in icy lines. Could we see through her sides, we should then behold four-and-twenty men parted off in two spaces under the suns of two lamps. Let us inspect them, and first the cabin of the officers in the after part of the ship.

2. Neither few nor slight were our struggles to remedy the various inconveniences which we encountered; their enumeration here is meant to aid the experience of future adventurers. Though our arrangements were far from complete or perfect, we had never to complain of the discomforts which previous expeditions, even the second German expedition to Greenland, had to endure from the

excessive condensation of moisture. Against this enemy we protected ourselves by the snow wall which we raised round the ship, by covering in the deck windows of the cabin, by lining our quarters with vulcanized india-rubber, by sheds built over the cabin stairs, all acting as condensers. Before, however, I enter on the unavoidable inconveniences to which we were exposed by the formation of ice, or by damp and the sudden

THE "TEGETTHOFF" IN THE FULL MOON.

change of temperature, I would preface my remarks by observing, that all these discomforts and inconveniences are to be endured far more easily than would seem possible to the reader, and that life on board a ship of a North-Pole expedition, under normal circumstances, is free from annoyances worthy of mention.

3. It is a matter of the last importance to keep the air pure and wholesome, and to maintain an equable warmth

in the quarters of the officers and crew. The accumulation of moisture and consequent congelation in them is an inconvenience which requires incessant watchfulness to avert.[1] The destruction of the snow wall which surrounded the ship increased the condensation; for that snow covering was nothing but a greatcoat for the ship and those on board. In the beginning of November 1872 the frost on the bulk-heads of the berths and on those parts of the cabins which were impervious to warmer air was very perceptible. The bed-clothes were frozen at night to the sides of the ship, the iron knees of the beams—not, alas! covered with felt—gleamed like stalactites, small glaciers were formed under the berths, and even in October the skylight was frozen inches thick. Every rise in the temperature caused this formation of ice to fall down like a "douche," and with the opening of a door a white vapour, even in October, streamed along the deck. We prevented the increase of moisture by cutting the openings in the deck, over which we placed two chimneys, each a foot high and covered with a thin metal cap. We boarded up the skylight, leaving a lid

[1] Parry mentions as a fact illustrative of the increase of moisture and its condensation into ice, that about a hundred hundredweights of ice were once removed from the lower quarters of the *Hecla*, which had accumulated there from the breath, the steam caused by cooking, and the moisture brought down by the clothes of the men.

by which to air the cabin. But in spite of all this the variations of temperature within our quarters were extraordinary. If the heat of the air in the middle of the cabin and on a level with our heads rose from $-15°$ to $+22°$ R.—our usual mean temperature—it amounted on the floor to a little above $+1°$, and fell during the night not unfrequently below freezing point.

4. But the greatest inconvenience perhaps with which we had to contend, arose from the removal of the protection of the tent roof, which was stretched over the after part of the ship. The want of this prevented our walking on the deck in bad weather, and it also hindered perfect ventilation, which could only be secured, with the constant heat which was maintained below, by keeping the deck windows open. Warming the air from underneath the floor of the cabin would possibly be preferable to the best stove. We had the stove of Meidinger of Carlsruhe, the excellence of which had been tested on the *Germania*. This stove consumed only 20 lbs. of coals daily, with a thermometer at $-20°$ R., and after the adoption of certain arrangements to save the fuel, its consumption amounted to only 12 lbs. Even in the coldest period of the winter we never consumed more than $4\frac{1}{2}$ cwt. in a month. The lighting of the mess-room and quarters of the men was effected by petroleum, the daily consumption of which amounted

to about $2\frac{2}{3}$ lbs. Altogether there were in the ship two large and two small lamps, besides the deck-lantern, which were burning day and night. The berths were lighted with train-oil; for special purposes, such as drawing, candles were used.

5. The stove had one troublesome enemy in the shape of a hole, as big as a man's head, in the door of the mess-room, through which a cold stream of air poured itself; and as the ship dipped forward considerably, and the hearth was only about a foot above the floor of the mess-room, this stream filled the whole space with a lake of cold air from three to four feet deep. Hence, while in the berth close by the stove there was a temperature ranging between + 30° and + 44° R., in the other, there was one which would have sufficed for the North Pole itself. In the former a hippopotamus would have felt himself quite comfortable, and Orel, the unhappy occupant of it, was often compelled to rush on deck, when the ice-pressures alarmed us, experiencing in passing from his berth to the deck a difference of temperature amounting to 70° R. In the other berth of the mess-room, water, lemon-juice, and vinegar froze on the floor. Those who occupied it, as they lay in beds, or those who sat at the table to read, were in a cold bath reaching up to their neck. But the hole was an indispensable necessity, for it was better to endure

the discomfort even of such a draught than to impede ventilation. Other causes, too, disturbed the equilibrium of temperature. At night the stove was sometimes, from sanitary considerations, not lighted, and then all had to sleep in that cold bath. With the increase of cold and wind, our inconveniences often assumed somewhat ludicrous forms. Some passages from my journal will make this clear:—" When any come below the temperature falls. If the door be opened there rolls in a mass of white vapour; if any one opens a book which he has brought with him, it smokes as if it were on fire. A cloud surrounds those that enter, and if a drop of water falls on their clothes, it is at once converted into ice, even at the stove. Frequently the upper stratum of air in the mess-room becomes so heated, that the deck light has to be opened, and then it rises up, like smoke out of a chimney, to blend itself with the cold air without."

6. The arrangements of the officers' mess-room are simple and in harmony with its purpose. Here stands a large table, used for study and for meals; the smaller berths, where the officers sleep, are round the sides of the mess-room—just large enough to enable a man to breathe in. There, in a recess between two pillars, an untold resource, the library (of about 400 volumes, chiefly scientific); close beside it the chronometers, and

lastly, the inevitable evils, the medical stores, ranged round the mast. By the side of scientific works stand Petermann's *Mittheilungen;* and between Milton's *Paradise Lost* and Shakespeare's immortal works, a whole tribe of romances, which were read with never-tiring delight. Our instruments, too, frosted with ice, are here, and a chest containing our journals. Once a month a cask, filled with wine—the chemical wine—concocted of snow, alcohol, tannin, sugar, and glycerine, was placed there. Dr. Kepes was not only our physician, but our wine brewer. One thing more we have to mention, which, alas! incommoded us much too little—wine; that is, wine made in Austria, from grapes. As we have already mentioned, the want of room in the cabin prevented our laying in a large stock, and the supplies we had were frozen in a cellar below the mess-room, about the middle of December, for the temperature of even this place was about $-7°$ or $-8°$ R. Each, however, had a bottle of rum as an allowance for eighteen days. But quite inexhaustible was the supply of our common drink—melted snow—a great jar of which, filled to the brim, stood always on the table. Under the cabin were our supplies of alcohol and petroleum, accessible only by well-fitting pipes, but possible volcanoes as far as our safety was concerned. From the accumulation of so many combustible materials, together with 20,000 cartridges, and with several lamps constantly burning, it is clear that the danger of fire was great. But once only had we an alarm from this source—when Carlsen caused us much trepidation by accidentally discharging a rifle in the cartridge magazine.

7. Let us now turn to the persons who occupied this mess-room. Marola, the steward, lights the lamp, and kindles the fire, and awakens those who were not already awoke by the smoke from the stove, with the cry, "Signori, le sette e tre quarti, prego d'alzarsi;" and after a pause of a quarter of an hour, during which the sleepers seem carefully to deny their existence, he startles this silence of indifference by the second call: "Colazion' in tavola." Out of every berth now comes forth its occupant, each in picturesque costume; costumes teach us how superficial after all is civilization in man!

8. The day's work begins. The watch, as ever, walks the deck, lest the ice should slip away from the world unobserved; in the mess-room meanwhile calculations or drawing or writing are in full operation. Our daily meals consist of a breakfast of cocoa, biscuit, and butter ; of a dinner of soup, boiled beef, preserved vegetables, and *café noir;* and of tea in the evening, with hard biscuit, butter, cheese, and ham. I would recommend *potage* instead of *tea* for the evening meal to all

future expeditions. Many of the articles of food must be thawed before the process of cooking begins, the greater part of the provisions being frozen as hard as iron. The tins with preserved meat stand for hours in boiling water, and the things for supper on the cabin stove, in order to be thawed. A plate of cheese that steams, butter as hard as a stone, which has thrown off the salt it contained in great lumps from the action of frost, a ham as hard as the never-thawed ground of the Tundra of Siberia, form an icy repast, specially if we use knives, which are so cold that they often break with the least exertion of force. I will here notice the sanitary importance—insisted on by Parry and Ross—of fresh bread, which the cook in an Arctic ship should be able to bake about twice a week. On board the *Tegetthoff* we used at first Liebig's "Baking-powder," but this from being kept too long gave such a disagreeable taste to the bread, that we gave it up and contented ourselves with a defective leaven.

9. Every Sunday at noon we celebrated Divine Service. Under the shelter of the deck-tent, the Gospel was read to the little band of Christians gathered together by the sound of the ship's bell, in all that grave simplicity which marked the worship of the early Christian Church. The Service over, we then sat down to the Sunday dinner, which was graced by a glass of wine and cake.

Carlsen and Lusina were our guests by turns. Carlsen always appeared in his wig, trimmed with extra care, and on the high festivals of the Church decorated also with the cross of the order of St. Olaf. Lusina, our excellent boatswain, was ready to talk with enthusiasm on any subject whatever, prefacing his stream of words

DIVINE SERVICE ON DECK.

with some sententious remark or with some far-fetched introduction. During our meals the conversation turned on our plans for the future; we talked of polar bears; we discussed the question of the existence of Gillis' Land and the possibility of our reaching Siberia; but very seldom did we venture to speak of what filled the minds of all—our captivity in the ice. Political combinations formed a favourite theme; and as we had some old numbers of the *Neue Frei Presse* on board, they furnished an inexhaustible source of topics for conversation. The events of the year 1870 were related as the latest news, and we thought anxiously of the issue of the war between Germany and France, and feared lest Austria should be compelled to take part in it.

10. After dinner came the hour for contemplation; in our lonely berths and by the side of our beds we sat down to brood—to listen to our watches beating seconds. The English Arctic expeditions, during the long period of their enforced leisure, found a great source of amusement and distraction in theatricals. But the ships of these expeditions had far larger crews than the *Tegetthoff*, and the men could be more easily spared for these recreations. But there were other reasons why we could not think of following the example of the English. Our situation during the first winter was far too serious for such things, and no other place for the theatre was at our disposal except the barricaded deck; and we should have had to sit there with a thermometer marking from 20° to 30° of cold, and see how the actors and the audience suddenly rubbed their frost-bitten feet with snow! There was one other potent reason for this renunciation—our performances must have been in four different languages.

11. Monotonous beyond all monotony is life in the long night of a Polar winter, and exile can never on earth be so entire as here under the dreadful triumvirate—darkness, cold, and solitude. In such a life, the man who surrenders himself to idleness, or even to sleeping during the day, must necessarily be utterly demoralized. In fact, nothing can be more destructive to an expedition wintering in the Arctic regions than the indulgence of mental or bodily lassitude. The real ground of the failure of the attempts made in earlier times to winter in Jan Mayen and other places in the far North was probably the utter want of discipline. There is, however, a widely spread, though mistaken view, that the long day of Polar lands is oppressive to man. Nothing is more untrue; for not continual light, but constant darkness, is distressing. Continual day-light heightens the energies and vital powers ; and yet, in our own first winter, it was less the darkness which wore us than the perpetual anxiety; when our greatest consolation was found in the Arabic proverb, "*In niz beguzared*" (*This too will pass away*), inscribed on our cabin wall.

12. After supper before going to bed, we smoked our cigars in the shed over the cabin steps, with a thermometer from 20° to 30° below zero R., and talked pleasantly over bygone days, though our thoughts were not unmixed with gloomy forebodings, as we heard ever

and anon the ominous sounds that issued from the moving ice. Existence on board a straining and groaning ship resembles life over a volcano. It was only after we had been some time in this ice-covered wooden grotto that the temperature rose, through our own heat, a few degrees, and it was certainly some testimony to the excellence of my down-quilted clothes, that I could wear them in the cabin without being distressed by the heat, and yet I was able to sit the whole evening in this freezing hole without suffering from cold. A train-oil lamp sends out almost more smoke than light, and when the snow drifted, we had to contend with the importunities of the dogs, who seemed to regard the deck shed as a great dog-kennel. With a sudden rise of the outer temperature this shed became utterly uninhabitable, for its coating of ice then melted and fell down like rain.

13. The effect of the long winter night is even greater on the body than on the mind, because of the insufficient opportunities for exercise. Middendorf contrasting the influence of climate on men remarks : "I consider travels in cold regions, even in the most unfavourable conditions of climate, to be far less dangerous to life than travels under the tropics. The former certainly are unutterably more miserable, but as certainly less deadly. I say this notwithstanding the danger which threatens ships when they penetrate

far within the realms of ice. We are never secure from sudden and deadly attacks of illness in tropical countries, but the longer we remain in them the less is the danger; whereas the high North deteriorates the constitution of the blood, and after three winters, very few can stand a fourth." To the influences of Polar life detrimental to health, must be added the constant hindrance to perspiration from wearing an extra quantity of woollen clothing, more or less hurtful as it is more or less waterproof, the want of fresh animal and vegetable food, and last, but not least, the periodic departure of light and warmth.

14. Our sanitary condition during the two winters we spent on board the *Tegetthoff* was not altogether satisfactory. Scorbutic affections of the mouth and diseases of the lungs appeared sometimes in distressing shapes, and scarcely a day passed in which we had not one or two on the sick list. I believe, however, that our trying situation had far more to do with these evils, than the southern blood and breeding of our people. The incessant watchfulness and care of Dr. Kepes left nothing undone, which could counteract the evil influences to which we were exposed. The berths of the crew were changed in rotation, and those which were exposed to the greatest accumulation of ice, were dried by warm air conveyed through movable pipes. Want of exercise, constant change of temperature, depression of mind, the

periodic scarcity of fresh meat, were the causes of the scurvy. In our first winter it appeared only in the more crowded quarters of the crew. It was then also that the first symptoms of lung-disease appeared in Krisch, the engineer, which he probably contracted from "catching cold." From that time he liked to sit by the stove and always complained of cold. Our supplies of preservatives against, and remedies for, scurvy were rather limited, although we had at our disposal several hundred tins of preserved vegetables, a cask of cloud-berries (*Rubus chamæmorus*), which we had brought from Tromsoe, and above a hundred bottles of lime juice. Wine also is an important preservative; we therefore served out to the crew, notwithstanding our small supply, twice a week, not Kepes' artificial, but real wine—at the rate of two bottles for eighteen men. No doubt scorbutic symptoms would have been far more general and severe, had we not been fortunate enough to shoot no less than sixty-seven polar bears, a larger number than had fallen to any previous expedition. It was more a sign of our good intentions to leave nothing undone or untried in our efforts against this malady, than any actual service it was to us, that we sowed cress and cabbage—radishes did not succeed—in a bed which we suspended over the stove. It was interesting, however, to observe how the little plants of cress, with every change of position, always turned to the light of the lamp, growing to the height of three inches, and in spite of their brimstone colour, retaining the true cress flavour.

15. The use of the bath tends greatly to promote health, for without it the skin of the body has no other stimulant; but the insecurity of our position rendered bathing sometimes a somewhat doubtful enjoyment. I remember many cases, when some of us, while bathing in the cold dark washing place in lukewarm water an inch deep, were alarmed by a sudden pressure of ice. Ultimately we gave up this practice, finding that it produced a troublesome amount of damp.

16. To a stranger, who should have visited us during this winter, nothing in the ship would have been so surprising and interesting as a visit to the quarters of the crew. Except for an hour, from five to six o'clock in the evening, when they were encouraged to take exercise in the open air, the rest of their time was spent in school, or in the duties of the watch, or in the work of the ship. Our supply of Slavonic books was unfortunately not very ample, and besides, not all the crew were able to read; the greater therefore was their tendency, like men of southern climes, to harmless noise, and I believe that some of our people, during the whole expedition, never ceased to speak. Here I beg to insert some passages

from my journal:—" Passing by the steaming kitchen, we enter their mess-room. Here in a narrow space we find the toilers of the sea and the mountains—eighteen in number. A little band of Dalmatians who for the first time encounter darkness and cold, the horrors of which are increased tenfold to men born and bred in the sunny South. Truly it could be no little thing to such men to be torn from sleep almost every night by the movement of the ice, to sit day after day in the long night of winter without any real intellectual occupation, and yet not to become demoralized, but remain calm and composed, and ever ready to obey and oblige. Can anything higher be said in their praise? Those men slept, each by himself, in a double row of berths; only Lusina the boatswain, and Carlsen the harpooner, who had circumnavigated Spitzbergen and Novaya Zemlya, occupied a separate partition. The clatter of the tongues of so many vehement Southerners was like the sound made by the smaller wheels of a machine, while the naïve simplicity of the grave Tyrolese came in between times, like the steady beat of a great cogwheel. It was a miniature reproduction of the confusion of tongues of Babel. Lusina speaks Italian to the occupants of the officers' cabin, English with Carlsen, French with Dr. Kepes, and Slavonic with the crew. Carlsen had adopted for the "Slavonians," as he called our people, a kind of speech compounded of Norwegian, English, German, Italian, and Slavonic. The crew, with the exception of the two Italians, speak Slavonic among themselves. The head of the little German colony is the cook, a Styrian; his heart is better than his culinary skill, for only too readily he leaves his work to be done by the stove. There is also among them a Moravian, Pospischill, the Vulcan of the ship; but we must return to the predominant race—the Slavonic. There is Lukinovich, a very Harpagon, always collecting, finding treasures in nails, empty bottles, lamp wicks, and searching even under the snow for articles wherewith to fill his sack— the sack which he was one day to leave behind him, much against the grain, when we abandoned the ship. There is Marola, the steward, and Fallesich, who had worked at the Suez Canal, these are our great singers. Then Palmich with his lance, the man whose zeal never bated, and whose very glance transfixed everything: Vecerina, the Job of the party, and the merry Titans, Sussich and Catarinich; Latkovich and Lettis, 'the philosophers;' Stiglich, the immovable confessor of passive obedience and the unlawfulness of resistance; Zaninovich, the "pearl;" Haller the herdsman and Klotz the prophet. Five of these men had run away from their wives. Klotz the prophet was under all circumstances, not indeed the most useful, but the most interesting person of this little community. A lofty calm worthy of an Evangelist graced his outer man; of still greater stature than Andreas Hofer, he wore, like him, a large black beard. As a hunter, a guide, a collector of stones, and a lonely enthusiast, he had moved about the mountains of his home, leading a life of visions. At home he was regarded as an incomparably bold mountaineer, and the ropes of the ship were to him so many convenient foot-paths. His reputation as a physician in his native land was great, and on board ship he failed not with his good offices. Haller, his fellow-countryman, shared with Klotz the office of armourer, and the duties of hunter and driver of the sledge dogs; and when we began our sledge journeys, both of them were ready to relieve others in dragging. Both had served in the army, Klotz on the Tonale, Haller on the Stelvio, and in 1868 the latter had been my useful companion, when I was engaged in the survey of the Ortler and Adamello Alps. "The philosophers" of our party, Latkovich and Lettis, had drawn a fine distinction between the different layers of ice, according as they contained a greater or less amount of saline matter: *Ghiaccio della prima* and *Ghiaccio della seconda qualità*.

17. To obviate as far as possible the evils of too much leisure among the men, a school was instituted at the

beginning of the January of the second year; Lieutenant Weyprecht, Brosch and Orel undertook the Italians and Slavonians, and I the Tyrolese. To avoid all confusion I retired with my smaller body of pupils to the shed on deck. Here, with the thermometer at 20° or 30° below zero R., the seed of wisdom was sown in the hearts of these sons of nature; but alas! the climate was not favourable to its growth. After many painful disillusions, the Pole was ascertained to be the intersection of lines in a point, of which nothing was to be seen in reality. If in this little lecture-room an exercise had to be examined, and the scholars were obliged to hold in their breath, in order that the teacher, who spoke out of a cloud, might be able to see the slate; or when the pupils engaged in a division sum had suddenly to stop to rub their hands with snow, was it a matter of wonder if the school did not flourish exceedingly?

18. The food of the crew consisted principally of preserved meats, different kinds of pulse, and the products of the chase, amounting on an average to two bears a week. Bear-flesh, roasted, was liked by all; the seal was at first despised, till necessity corrected taste. Besides artificial wine, water was their strongest drink.

CHAPTER VII.

ICE PRESSURES.

1. WHEN compared with the tortures we endured from the thought that we were captives in the ice, little to us seemed the dangers which threatened our existence, though these assumed the appalling form of ice pressures. Daily almost the ship had to sustain the attacks of our old enemy, and when the ice seemed to repose, threatening indications were not wanting to warn us how short that repose might be. My journal records a long series of commotions in the ice on almost every day of January 1873, and even during the pauses the timbers of the ship continually shook and trembled and creaked. The pressures accompanied by a low grumbling noise were very great on the 3rd, and lasted till the oldest ice was shattered, during which our hatchways were displaced. On the 4th the pressures continued without intermission during the whole day. But on the 22nd they exceeded all we had hitherto experienced. When we awoke in the morning, the crashing of the masses of ice was

dreadful. In the mess-room we heard a deep, grumbling, rumbling noise—the ship trembled like a steam vessel under very high pressure. When we hastened on deck we were greeted by the long howls which issued from the ice, and we were soon convinced of the exceedingly

ICE PRESSURE IN THE POLAR NIGHT.

formidable character of this special onset! Ten paces astern of the ship, the ice had been heaved up in a moment into mountains. With the greatest difficulty, amid the profound darkness that prevailed, the boats were got on board, and many stores re-shipped, though some of our coals had to be sacrificed. A tent formed of sails was engulfed, and our water-hole utterly displaced by the pressures; it was only after many attempts that we succeeded in finding a thinner ice-table, which we pierced till we found water. January 26, again tremendous pressures roused us from sleep. In half an hour every preparation was made to leave the ship, and I believe that many of us, while waiting the issue amid the fearful din heard from the deck, longed that the ship might be crushed, in order to escape from the torture of continually preparing to depart.

2. I will not, however, fatigue the reader with the monotonous rehearsal of our ever-recurring daily dangers, but will here insert a few passages from my journal of that date which will suffice to explain our position:—

"Scarcely asleep after the exhaustion and cares of the day, the timbers of the ship begin to moan and groan close by our ear, and we awake and lie listening to the onset of the ice. We hear the step of the watch on deck crackling on the ice as he paces to and fro; as long as it is measured and steady we know there is nothing to be feared. Again that uncanny creaking in the timbers, and the watch comes to announce to those below that the terrible movement in the ice has begun, and once more we all spring from our beds, put on our fur clothes, seize our ready-filled bags, and amid the darkness stand ready on deck, and listen to the war between the ice and the elements. In autumn, when the ice-fields were not nearly so large as in the winter, their collision was accompanied by a deep dull sound ; but now, rendered hard and brittle by the extreme cold, a sound as of a howl of rage [1] was emitted as they crashed together. Ever nearer come the rushing, rattling sounds, as if a thousand heavy waggons were driving over a plain. Close under us the ice begins to tremble, to moan and wail in every key ;—as the fury of the conflict increases, the grumbling becomes deeper and deeper, concentric fissures open themselves round the ship, and the shattered portions of the floes are rolled up into heaps. The intermitting howls become fearfully rapid, announcing the acme of the conflict, and anxiously we listen to the sound which we know too well. Then follows a crash and crack, and many dark lines wander over the ice : these are for a moment narrow fissures, the next moment they yawn asunder like abysses. Often with such a crash the force of the pressure seems broken ; the piles of ice collapse, like the undermined walls of a fortress, and calm is again restored. But to-day this was but the commencement, and with renewed violence a second assault of the ice begins, then a third, yea a fourth. Tables of ice broken off from the floes around us rise perpendicularly

---

[1] The noise produced by such collisions cannot be more fittingly expressed.

from the sea ; some are bent under the enormous pressure, and their curved shapes attest the elasticity of ice. Like a giant in the conflict, a veteran floe, many winters old, crushes in its rotations its feeble neighbours, and in turn succumbs to the mighty iceberg—the leviathan of all ice-forms, which forces its way through a phalanx of opposing masses, crushing them to pieces as it advances. And in this wild and fearful tumult a ship—squeezed, pressed, all but crushed, by the ice; her crew on deck, ready to leave her at a moment's notice. Boats and sledges, tents, provisions, arms and ammunition, everything prepared, if the ship should at last be destroyed—but for what? for an escape? no one really thought this possible, though all were ready for the attempt. But again the conflict ceases, and once more we breathe freely, and can contemplate the wonderful change that has come on everything round us. A few minutes have sufficed to create a maze of mountain chains from a plain of ice. The flat surfaces covered with snow, which we saw yesterday, are gone. Ice ruins are visible on every side. Abysses gape between the shattered masses, and show the dark sea beneath. Gradually a calm has crept over all; equilibrium is reinstated in the desolate realm of ice ; new "leads" and "ice-holes" have been opened up, but for the *Tegetthoff* no liberation."

CHAPTER VIII.

THE WANE OF THE LONG POLAR NIGHT.

1. ALTHOUGH the sun was mounting higher, there was no essential change in the gloom and darkness which surrounded us. In fact we were drifting during the whole of January towards the north, and were wintering nearer the pole than any who had ever preceded us.[1] On gloomy days, noon was not distinguishable. We were now four hundred miles within the Frozen Ocean, and had been for five months the sport and play of winds and currents, and nothing indicated any change in our situation. Yet, in spite of our desperate position, the first, ever so faint, indications of the return of light filled us with joy. With a clear atmosphere, January 10, we observed for the first time at noon a decided brightness, and on the 19th a brilliant carmine was seen in the sky, an hour before noon on the southern horizon. After a long obscuration from cloudy weather, the

[1] Hall's contemporaneous expedition excepted.

morning twilight increased gradually, and by the end of the month it was discernible in the forenoon. As the light increased, the signs of the convulsions were more distinctly seen. Round us there rose piles of craggy ice, which, hurled up, as from a crater, by the ice-pressure of the 22nd, kept us in a state of constant fear, lest the ice-walls would break up and fall in upon us. At a little distance off, nothing was to be seen of the ship but the tops of its masts: the rest of it was hidden behind a lofty wall of ice. The ship itself, raised seven feet above the level of the sea rested on a protuberance of ice, and, removed from its natural element, looked a truly miserable object. This ice protuberance had been formed from a floe which had been often rent asunder and frozen again, and had been rounded in a singular manner from the underdriving of the ice and the lateral pressure in its recent movements. In other respects, also, our environment had been completely changed. Before the movement in the ice on the 22nd, a narrow strip of level ice wound like a river through a maze of hummocks, and throughout the winter this had been diligently used for exercising the dogs. Of this nothing was now to be seen: walls of ice rose, where a fortnight before our coal-house had stood; fissures gaped on every side. In every respect the weather during this month was capricious and unaccountable. In the first two weeks, the temperature fell several times below 30° R., and on January 8, 13 and 14, quicksilver, exposed to the cold, froze to a solid mass; gin also froze, and alcohol only maintained its fluid state. Yet, notwithstanding this low temperature, the snow was always soft; and it continued to be so, amid all the variations of temperature and the high winds of this month. January 22 and 23, the temperature rose for a short time to − 2·8° R.; everything in the ship then began to thaw, and a disagreeable moisture penetrated both our clothes and our quarters. The mean temperature of this month, in consequence of these abnormal variations, did not exceed − 18° R., and was therefore about ten degrees higher than might have been expected.

2. The bears had in these last weeks kept at a regrettable distance from us. On the 12th however, a very large fellow ventured to come within ten paces of the rope ladder on the starboard side. We fired at him with explosive balls and he fell; but his strength was so great that even after these terrible wounds he was able to get up and run. Explosive bullets, however, are to be recommended for encounters with bears, though their flight is rather uncertain. A bear hunt, on the 29th and 30th, had a somewhat tragical result. About ten o'clock at night, when it was quite dark, a bear approached the ship, and with the agility of a tiger

fell on Sumbu, who got away very cleverly and by his loud barking summoned Krisch, who was then on watch, to his aid. When he was not more than ten feet from the deck Krisch fired at him and wounded him. The noise brought some of us at once, and though it was exceedingly dark and the snow very deep, a useless chase, in which I joined, forthwith began. The pursuit through the midst of driving snow became weaker; until at last I found myself alone with Palmich. We could see nothing and heard only an occasional howl of pain. We hastened our steps through the whirling snow, till we saw, by the dim light of our lantern, Matoschkin lying howling on the ground, and the bear a few steps from him, vigorously assailed by Sumbu, who seized him by the foot whenever he began to retreat. As Matoschkin incautiously approached too near, the bear turned, seized him, and carried him off. To fire with effect was impossible; we were too far off to take aim with our rifles. The bear continued to drag the dog along, and at last a puff of wind put out our lantern, and we soon discovered our inability to keep up with our enemy. Bitterly as we lamented the fate of the poor dog, whose howls were brought to our ears by the wind, we had nothing for it but to return to the ship. About noon next day when it was sufficiently clear, Brosch, the two Tyrolese, and I set out to ascertain the fate of the

PHIDIAS AT WORK UPON THE ATHENA

dog. The snow was drifting heavily, and we constantly sank into it as we advanced. After a toilsome walk we came on traces of blood, which Sumbu followed up, while Gillis timidly stuck to us. At last, after we had gone on for the third of a mile, Sumbu came back in a great state of excitement, and then ran on before us till he stopped at an ice-hummock, where he renewed his angry barks. We advanced with quickened steps and with our rifles cocked, and when we were about twenty paces from it the bear came out from behind, apparently in great astonishment. After several shots the bear fell, but again gathering himself up he dragged himself along like a walrus, in spite of his broken spine, with extraordinary activity towards an "ice-hole" covered with young ice. Two other shots with explosive bullets terminated his career, and Matoschkin, whose body we afterwards found behind the ice-hillock, was avenged.

3. The cold set in with great intensity with the month of February and maintained itself throughout it: the mean monthly temperature being $-28°$ R. Repeatedly the quicksilver froze, and in the last eight days it remained solid. Even the petroleum was frozen on the 17th at $-36°$ R. in the globe of the lamp, though it was throwing out a considerable heat. The lowest temperature we experienced was on the last day of the month.

—37° R. Notwithstanding the extreme cold, the light had increased so much, that a thermometer, in which the degrees were strongly marked, could be read off, even on the 3rd of the month, at ten o'clock in the forenoon without the aid of lamplight; and on the 20th we were able to carry on our meteorological observations, without any artificial light at six o'clock in the evening. The ruddiness we observed at noon in the south grew more and more decided. On clear days we could discern, about seven o'clock in the morning, a faint twilight, and at noon of February 14 the near approach of the sun was distinctly to be traced by a bright cloud that was resting over it, though it was still below the horizon. About the middle of the month, there was light enough to cause the different forms and groups of ice to cast shadows. In spite of the low temperature, we remained for hours in the open air, though previously to this period we had ventured on deck for a few minutes only at a time—the watch of course excepted. But as the daylight increased, we saw also what a dark, gloomy grave had been our abode for so long a period. All our thoughts and conversations were concentrated on the returning light of the sun. The movements of the ice ceased to be a source of dread, though for several days during the month they had been exceedingly formidable. In the course of our drifting we had penetrated into a region where never ship had been before. The following table exhibits the course of the *Tegetthoff*, as she drifted from August 21, 1872, to February 27, 1873.

Time.	N. Lat.	E. Lon.	Time.	N. Lat.	E. Lon.
Aug. 21, 1872, day when the ship was beset	° ′ 76·22	° ′ 62·3	Nov. 9, 1872 „ 14 „ „ 18 „	° ′ 78·15 78·8 78·10	° ′ 69·42 71·16 70·31
Sept. 1, 1872	76·25	62·50	„ 28 „	78·13	69·48
„ 4 „	76·23	62·49	Dec. 4 „	78·19	69·1
„ 11 „	76·35	60·18	„ 8 „	78·21	69·2
„ 14 „	76·37	60·50	„ 12 „	78·25	68·57
„ 21 „	76·28	63·9	„ 16 „	78·22	67·42
„ 26 „	76·36	64·8	„ 19 „	78·13	67·11
„ 27 „	76·38	64·4	„ 26 „	78·10	68·19
„ 28 „	76·37	64·10	Jan. 2, 1873	78·37	66·56
Oct. 1 „	76·50	65·22	„ 19 „	78·43	69·32
„ 2 „	76·59	65·48	„ 26 „	78·50	71·47
„ 3 „	77·4	66·1	Feb. 2 „	78·45	73·7
„ 17 „	77·50	69·22	„ 14 „	78·12	72·20
„ 18 „	77·48	69·8	„ 19 „	78·15	71·38
„ 22 „	77·46	69·26	„ 23 „	79·11	
„ 31 „	77·53	69·12	„ 27 „	79·12	
Nov. 5 „	77·53	69·30			

4. The inspection of this table shows that the movement of the ship was retarded as the increasing cold closed the open places of the sea, and when we fell under the influence of the Siberian ice-drift from east to west. It may be remarked, too, that we drifted generally straight before the wind, and that we and our floe during the first four months turned only one degree in azimuth. By the end of January all the open places of the sea were closed; and the masses of ice were

thus driven one over the other from their mutual pressure, and pile thus rose upon pile. It seems probable, also, that wind was the main cause of our drifting, while sea currents were only of secondary moment. From the beginning of the month of February we drifted constantly toward the north-west, and from this deviation in our course, we indulged in the hope that we were approaching the mysterious Gillis' Land. But at this time the liberation of the ship in the summer was the sum of our expectations and desires. In fact there was not one of us who doubted this eventuality. Fully convinced, as we were, that our floes, firmly attached to each other, would ultimately break up and drift southwards, we determined to make them the bearers of the record of what had befallen us. Hence we threw out, February 14th, round the ship a number of bottles, inclosing a narrative of the main events of the expedition from the departure of Count Wilczek up to that date.

CHAPTER IX.

THE RETURN OF LIGHT.—THE SPRING OF 1873.

1. Though the sun did not return to our latitude (78° 15', 71° 38' E. long.) till the 19th of February, we were able to greet his beams three days previous to that date, owing to the strong refraction of 1° 40', which accompanied a temperature of − 30° (R.). To the polar navigator the return of the sun is an event of indescribable joy and magnificence. In those dreadful wastes he feels the force of the superstitions of past ages, and becomes almost a worshipper of the eternal luminary. As of old the worshippers of Belus watched its approach on the luxuriant shores of the Euphrates, we, too, standing on mountains of ice or perched on the masts of the ship, waited to hail the advent of the source of light. At last it came! A wave of light rolled through the vast expanse of heaven, and then—uprose the sun-god, surrounded with purple clouds, and poured his beams over the world of ice. No one spoke for a

time. Who indeed could have found words to embody the feelings of relief which beamed on the faces of all, and which found a kind of expression in the scarcely audible exclamation of one of the simplest and least cultured of the crew, "Benedetto giorno!" The sun had risen with but half his disk, as if reluctant to shine on a world unworthy of his beams. A rosy hue suffused the whole scene, and the cold Memnon pillars of ice gave forth mysterious whispers in the flood of heat and light. Now indeed with the sun had a new year begun—what was it to bring forth for us and our prospects? But alas his stay was short—he remained above the horizon for a few minutes only; again his light was quenched, and a hazy violet colour lay over distant objects, and the twinkling stars shone in the heavens.

2. While we watched the sun's return, we had also an opportunity of looking on each other. How shocked and surprised were we with the change which had been wrought on us in the long polar night! Our sunken cheeks were overspread with pallor; we had all the signs of convalescence after a long illness—the sharp-pointed nose, the sunken eye. The eyes of all had suffered from the light of lamps which had burnt for months; those especially who had used them for hard work. But all these consequences were of short duration under the beneficent influence of the daylight and the

spring sun, which soon brought colour into our faces. Cheerfulness gradually returned to all on board the *Tegetthoff*, as we revelled in the warm beams of the sun. We built a house of ice without a roof, and open to the south, and thither the healthy and the sick on calm fine days used to repair from the dreary ship, and sun themselves like lizards. But within the ship it was still night.

3. The visits of bears again became numerous. February 17th one of about five feet long was shot very close to the ship, and two days afterwards a second came near us, but was scared away by the awkwardness of the hunters. The dogs however pursued him, and we were compelled from fears for their safety to follow up the chase. The temperature of $-29°$ R., and a pretty strong wind against which we had to run in the pursuit brought on in some of our party palpitation of the heart and spitting of blood, and our return to the ship was a matter of some difficulty. On the morning of the 20th another bear came close to the ship, was fired at, but missed, and got away. Palmich, Haller, and Klotz immediately gave chase, though the temperature was $-32°$ R., and the wind high. After a short time Palmich returned with his face frost-bitten, and the Tyrolese after several hours, without any success, but with their feet so frost-bitten that they had

lost all feeling in them. The second stage of the malady had begun, which renders amputation almost a necessity. For several hours their feet had to be rubbed with snow till sensation returned, and with returning sensation much suffering; large swellings as big as a man's fist rose on their feet, which were reduced only after the application of ice for several days. Again, in the grey of the morning of February 22nd a bear came within eighty paces of the ship, which Sussich, the watch on deck, after several shots, which the animal seemed not in the least to regard, at last hit and killed. By a wound on his right forepaw we recognised our friend whom we had hotly chased a few days before. He was six feet in length, and in his stomach there was nothing but a small piece of the skin of a seal. Sussich was overjoyed with his success, and for the whole day tried to drag everyone outside the ship to show the result of his prowess. "Se mi non era, il copava tutti," he added, with a look of contempt on those who had not been so successful as himself.

4. Although at the end of February, the sun rose with a carmine light which imparted an indescribable charm to the fields of snow and ice, we were doomed to disappointment in our expectation of bright and clear weather in the after-part of the day. Soon after

sunrise, white frosty mists gathered over the ice-fields, making the sun as he shone through them a mere ball of light, or completely concealing him. On February 24th we enjoyed the peculiar spectacle of seeing the sun appear, the temperature being −34° R., distorted

THE CARNIVAL ON THE ICE.

by refraction, through the thick mists on the horizon, as if he were quite flat, beamless, and of a coppery red. The end of February reminded us of the carnival time of the land of the South, and the crew appeared in such masques as they could command; but their masquerading formed a sad and mocking contrast with the

R 2

gravity of our position. The men bestowed all their art on "Sumbu," who was dressed up as the demon "Lindwurm," and deported himself in a manner highly becoming his costume.

5. With the month of March the spring had, in name at least, begun; but in our sense of the word no spring as yet appeared. Instead of the joyous gleams of early vegetation, a blinding white waste environed us; instead of the perfumed breath of flowers and the soft air of spring, there rose driving clouds of ice-needles; and parhelia of almost daily occurrence shone in a heavy sleepy fashion through white frosty mists. The atmosphere was filled with snow; to be convinced of this we had only to look at the sun when the weather seemed clear and bright. This continual fall of snow as fine as dust, was the cause of the retardation of the evaporation of the ice. The influence of the sun was so great, that March 3 the black-bulb thermometer indicated the unusual temperature of $+ 6°$ R., and a layer of snow on the bows of the vessel showed evident signs of diminution. The thermometer, in the sun, rose eight degrees March 6, and nine degrees two days after. The weather was calm and clear, and the increasing influence of the sun was a most joyful sensation. A cube of ice freely suspended showed during the second half of March a daily diminution of $\tau\delta\sigma$ of its weight from evaporation; while

in the sea itself its behaviour was the very opposite; the cube of ice, which was submerged to a depth of ten feet from February 19th to March 5th, showed at the latter date an increase of its mass, amounting to ¾ of an inch round its surface. In the beginning and end of March the cold was so severe, that the thermometer every day for three weeks marked $-30°$ R. Calms and clear weather, however, characterized this period of the spring, and snow-drifting and a clouded sky were rare. On the 13th of March the full moon again appeared in the azure twilight of the western heavens, and its soft light fringed with silver the dark ranges of ice. The days became longer, and the shadows cast by the masses of ice were shorter and more marked, and every one who remained long in the open air was forced to use snow spectacles. Small avalanches began to fall from the rigging, and the masts, spars, and ropes lost their white frosted aspect. On the 22nd the fore part of the ship's hull facing the south was completely free from snow and its dark colour was visible. On the 29th the temperature in the sun exceeded the temperature at 9.30 A.M. by $15°$ R.; and on the 30th we could for the first time observe the melting of the snow on the seams of the timber of the ship's hull. The enumeration of these events, insignificant as they may appear, will serve to show, with what attention the polar navigator notes the minutest occurrence due to the influence of the sun.

6. Welcome, though illusive, harbingers of the returning summer were the first birds, whose arrival we greeted on the 19th. These were little divers, which flew over the ship to the open spaces of water amid the ice, there to seek their food in the countless crustaceæ which abound in them. Magnificent auroras continued to illuminate our nights; and although the duration of their intensity was much too brief to serve as a source of light, there was a charm in these phenomena which their daily recurrence could not weaken.

7. While under these various influences the health of all on board the *Tegetthoff* greatly improved, we were threatened with the serious calamity of losing our excellent physician, Dr. Kepes, who fell ill on the 13th of the month. For two weeks we were kept in a state of anxious fear for him; and our anxieties were increased as we had to treat his malady without the necessary knowledge and experience. To our great joy, however, he was spared to us; and our supply of fresh bear's-flesh was henceforth reserved for him.

8. For some time the bears had observed a very distressing reserve and shyness in their visits. On the 15th one came near us, and as Pekel had for some

time announced his approach, he found a long front of rifles drawn up behind some masses of ice to give him a warm reception. He, as usual, came on under the wind, showing considerable interest in our edifices. He then ascended a small ice-crag, and, after balancing himself carefully, sat down on the

THE "TEGETTHOFF" DRIFTING IN PACK ICE. MARCH 1873

top of it, with his snout uplifted, snuffing all round. This seemed so ludicrous to some of our party that they burst out into a laugh so loud, that the bear came down from his pinnacle in evident astonishment, and with much circumspection drew nearer and nearer till at a short distance from us he fell mortally wounded.

He was, alas! a very small animal, about 5½ feet long, and his stomach was absolutely empty. On the 30th of March another came close to the ship; the watch on shore fired at, but missed him, whereupon both the watch and the bear took to flight.

9. April at last arrived, and with it the time of icicles, which hung down from every yard of the ship, and from every rope of the rigging, from every icy ridge and crag. The melting and decaying of the ice, though always a source of satisfaction when the question of its breaking up is discussed, went on, to our impatient desires, with intolerable slowness. What was it to us that we were able to read even at midnight on the 2nd of April; that the number of divers and sea-gulls constantly increased; that on the 6th the difference of temperature between sun and shade was 18°; that the black-bulb thermometer on the 20th showed $+5°$ R.; that the sun on the 11th rose about two o'clock in the morning, and from the 16th remained constantly in the heavens? What did all this matter? The constant light notwithstanding, we were still environed with the signs of deepest winter, and the forms and masses of ice collapsed with a slow deliberation that tortured us. We were no longer to be satisfied and amused with the spectacle of parhelia, even though the phenomenon should appear, as it did on the 1st of April, with eight suns. Months of weary waiting still

lay before us; daily we had to arm ourselves with patience, as, when we came on deck, we discovered the apparently unchangeable character of our environment, with all its forms, which had become familiar to us down to the smallest details. Reluctantly condemned to almost total idleness, we filled up our time with such occupations as fancy suggested. Some of our people built a tower of ice on a level part of our floe; others tried their rifles—tried often enough before—at empty bottles as targets. Along with the Tyrolese I constructed a road through hills of ice, over passes and ridges, going up and down in serpentine paths, making a circuit of about three miles round the ship. The labour of weeks with picks and shovels was expended in making and preserving it; after each downfall of snow this road had to be dug out afresh. Our passing and repassing along it through a maze of ice not only beneficially exercised our bodies, but furnished opportunities for training our dogs to drag heavy-laden sledges. I continued also to fill my portfolio with studies of scenery in the ice, and I accustomed myself, whenever there was no wind, whatever might be the temperature, to draw for hours together with no other protection to my hands than light gloves.

10. April had begun with a temperature of $-31°$ R.; as the month advanced it steadily increased. At the end of

the month the extreme of cold was but – 15° R. But the weather had now lost the clearness of the early spring; and constant calms, together with the frequent falls of snow, undid the work of the few hours of the day on which the sun shone. The ice was covered with deep snow; on the level we sank ankle deep, while among the hummocks it was up to our knees. Sledging, would have been impracticable. Among the changes produced by the softening of the weather, none was greater or more agreeable than the return of daylight to the cabin, when we took off the covering of the skylight and removed the tent-roof from the fore part of the ship. Once more to be able to read without the dull glimmer of artificial light was an extraordinary event in our monotonous life. For five months our lamps had been burning in our messroom, so that the walls were black with smoke, and it was a work of no small labour to make them clean and pleasant. The unloading of the ship's hold was, however, a far heavier, though necessary task; the thick crusts of ice which had accumulated on its sides must be removed, lest the provisions should be damaged by their thawing; and there was no time to lose, for the temperature in the hold was only 1° below zero. The provisions, which had been left out on the ice, were again stowed in the ship, the cessation of the ice-pressures rendering this precautionary measure useless.

11. Round a ship which has wintered in the ice there is gradually accumulated a mass of rubbish of all kinds, of which cinders form a considerable constituent. These, when thrown out in small quantities, sink at once into the snow, while larger quantities act as a non-conducting layer. Hence we were surrounded by a maze of holes, big and little, alternating with plateaus, under which winter still continued to linger. When thaw-water made its appearance, all this was transformed into a succession of lakes and islands, which we bridged over by planks.

12. Meantime we began our labours of digging out the ship. We removed the wall of snow, which had served as an outer garment and protection during the winter, and the hard-trodden layer which covered the deck a foot thick. In clearing away from the after-part of the ship, we discovered that the machinery protecting the screw had been torn away by the ice-pressures. The mischief done, however, was not considerable; and as the ship made no water, we consoled ourselves with the thought, that she had sustained no material injury, though she had lain so long out of water perched on the floe.

13. The continued cessation of movements in the ice induced Weyprecht to erect a tent at no great distance

from the ship, to carry on in it observations of the magnetic constants, which were taken on certain appointed days. On the night of one of such days, Orel, who conducted these observations, was surprised by the visit of a bear. His shouts for help brought us on deck, but before we could actually reach him, the seaman on the watch had killed the bear with an explosive bullet. Hitherto these animals had shown little courage in the neighbourhood of the ship, and to shoot them from the deck exposed no one to any danger; but this incident showed us that we could not count securely on their actions. Soon after this we had another surprise. Stiglich, the seaman on watch on shore, suddenly found himself confronted with a bear about eight paces off. Throwing his cap to the bear, he made a rush for the rope ladders of the ship, but fell in his hurry and confusion. Carlsen, hearing his cries for help, hastened to the rescue, and dexterously shot the pursuer. A glorious event for Carlsen! who used to tell us strange stories of his encounters with bears; how he had scared them away with the glance of his eye; and how once in Novaya Zemlya he had frightened away a whole pack of them by the magic of his glance. All doubts in the prowess of his eye were silenced to-day by the more unquestionable prowess of his rifle. On the 28th of May a bear clambering over the wall of ice close astern of the ship was shot dead with an explosive bullet. His stomach was empty, but notwithstanding his leanness, he furnished more meat than many others, for he was fully seven feet long.

14. At the end of April the force of the winds so loosened the compactness of the ice, that dark strips hanging above the horizon in all directions announced the existence of numerous fissures, although they were invisible even from the masts of the ship. We counted on these signs with such unshaken confidence, that when on the 2nd of May we heard in the distance the now familiar sound of the ice-pressures, we heard them not only without dismay, but as the voice of a joyous message. Three-quarters of a year had passed away since we were first caught in the ice—a time laden to us with bitter disappointments to our hopes, and great dangers to our lives. The hour of our long and ardently desired liberation seemed at hand. If once we got free, it lay within the bounds of possibility that we might reach, if not the somewhat mythical Gillis' Land, then at least the uninhabited arctic coasts of Siberia. Siberia had, in fact, become the rosiest of our hopes. Some, indeed, still indulged in extravagant expectations and counted on the discovery of new lands, even while they drifted with the ice. But our wishes for the most part had become so subdued, that the discovery of the

smallest cliff would have satisfied our ambition as discoverers.

15. But Nature's laws held their own course, undisturbed by our desires. Snow continued to fall in abundance, and spread its mantle over the ice. The constant round of downfalls and evaporation was a sad bar to our hopes. In the beginning of May the snow began to thaw on the surface, and became soft and sticky. Even in the depth of winter it was never hard, but like the fine dry grains of driving sand. This change in the snow, which occurs a fortnight earlier than in Greenland, compelled us to substitute our black leather boots for those of sailcloth, which we had hitherto worn. On the 2nd of May the temperature fell 18° below zero (R.), but it now began to rise gradually, so that it sometimes reached the zero point about the end of the month, and on the 29th rose two degrees above it. The mean temperature of the month, however, was not above $-7°$ R. But the difference of temperature in the sun and the shade became greater and greater. The thermometer marked $-22°$ R at 6 P.M. of the 1st of May, and on the 11th the black-bulb thermometer showed $+26°$ R. at 3 P.M., while the common instrument gave only -8 R. In the middle of the month, after the heavy winds fell, we were enveloped with dark fog banks; stray beams of the sun broke through the warm misty atmosphere, and

dark skies were succeeded by masses of white vapour illuminated by the sun. Just as in our happier clime, the Arctic April has her alternations of cloud and sunshine.

16. Hitherto the only birds which had visited us were divers and gulls. Once only a snow-bunting flew among us, and fearlessly settled on the ship. On the 24th of May the auks made their appearance, and from that date we were constantly entertained by the whirring sounds of their flight. As they keep one direction in their flight, we could shoot those only which passed over the ship; they were a useful addition to our table, though they had to be steeped in vinegar to make them palatable. The majestic Burgomaster Gull appeared somewhat later, and later still the "Ice-birds" frequented the shores of the lakes around us, and hovered round the remains of the bears we had shot. These birds settled with the greatest boldness in the immediate neighbourhood of the ship, and day and night filled the air with their wild shrill cries.

17. By the middle of March, Krisch, the engineer, had put the steam machinery in working order, but another month elapsed before the screw-propeller, which had been frozen fast, was set free; our fears lest it should refuse to act proved to be groundless. As however, there was no prospect of our being able to

use steam for some time, it was thought advisable to dig out and raise the rudder in order to secure it.

18. On the 26th of May a partial eclipse of the sun was visible in our latitude ; but from an error in our calculations, we had ante-dated the commencement of the observation by about two hours and a half. Everyone on board who had an instrument at his command stood ready to observe the passage of the moon over the sun's disk. After waiting for some time in vain, we discovered the error we had committed as to the time of the beginning of the eclipse, but in order that the dignity of astronomical observation might not be degraded in the eyes of the crew, we still held our ground with the telescopes in our hands. Two hours of such suspense enabled us to feel that there could be no more perfect fulfilment of the punishment of Sisyphus than being condemned to wait for an eclipse of the sun which would not come off! At last the eclipse took place, but not until great disgust had been excited in the minds of men, who were too much inclined to regard the whole thing as a piece of humbug. At the height of the eclipse about one-third only of the sun's disk was obscured, and the sun was so covered with mist that we could look at it without the use of coloured glasses. The whole duration of the eclipse was one hour and fifty-six minutes.

19. From the 1st of the month the number of living

creatures belonging to the expedition had been increased by the birth of four Newfoundland puppies, who passed the earliest days of their youth in a tent erected on the ice, and artificially heated to the temperature of a European May. But all our care in rearing this litter was frustrated by one of these little polar wretches, who, after sucking his mother till he was as round as a drum, lay on his brothers as they slept, and stifled them. This little criminal received the name of Torossy, and soon became the pet of the crew, and a favourite with all the other dogs. The fame which he afterwards gained made him an important member of the expedition. All the dogs had become so hardy during the past winter, that they now slept outside their kennels, finding the inside too warm for them.

CHAPTER X.

THE SUMMER OF 1873.

1. THE time crept away with indescribable monotony. The crew performed their heavy labours, but of events there were none. The only change in our position was the constant decay of the buttresses and walls of ice, until the frozen sea lay like a snowy chaos before us. Pure sharp-edged ice was nowhere to be seen; the edges were no longer transparent; evaporation had transformed the surface into a kind of glacier-snow. June 1, we had the greatest degree of cold of the month, the thermometer marking $-8.6°$ R.; but on the last day it rose to $+0.1°$ R.; the mean temperature being $-0.4°$ R. Every week brought us promises of summer. On the 1st the black-bulb thermometer reached $+29°$ R.; on the 14th rain fell for the first time; on the 16th the temperature, at 9 o'clock A.M., was $+4.2°$ R., on the 26th, $+6.4°$ R., and on the 29th even $+8.1°$ R. On these days the air seemed to have the

pleasant mildness of southern climes, and when there was no wind we felt an oppressive sultriness. Wreaths of mist moved along the icy wastes which glowed with sun-light, while the long dark lines of ice-wall lay in deep shadow. The air was filled with flocks of birds; day and night we heard the shrill cries of the Robber-gulls, ever and anon mingled with the barking of the dogs in full pursuit of them. Flocks of rotges congregated without fear in the narrow basins of distant "leads;" and the "great gulls," shunning companionship, sat for hours on the top of an ice-cliff, or in the middle of a floe.

2. No one who has not actually seen it, can imagine the blaze of light in the Arctic regions on clear days, or the glow which floats sometimes over the cold white ice-floes, with their outlines in constant vibration, while refraction transforms the ice-bergs into a variety of shapes. The sun's power is sometimes so great as to blister the skin in a few hours, and the glare from snow and ice produces snow-blindness, if the eyes be not carefully protected. At a little distance the sea appears to be of a deep black colour, though it still preserves its ultramarine hues in the narrow "leads;" even the pure blue of the heavens may be called almost black when compared with the dazzling

sheen of the ice. In the middle of June there was an incessant dripping and oozing in the ice-world, and streams of thaw-water flowed into the open fissures. By the end of the month the surface of the ice resembled snow; and even at some depth it was viscous, instead of brittle and hard as glass, as it is during the colder season. Streams of thaw-water ran through the softened and saturated snow. Small lakes were formed on the levels, and swamps of snow, wearing a traitorous exterior, surrounded their borders. In the summer of 1873 we observed a vertical decrease of five or six feet in the thickness of the ice; but this diminution in thickness was from the surface downwards, while in the sea itself, there was little or no thawing, because the temperature of its surface was still below zero. The moisture, from which there was no escape, became exceedingly troublesome. In spite of our stout leather boots we had never the comfort of dry feet during the whole of the summer, and this we felt the more, as our labours to free the ship, which we had commenced at the beginning of May, necessitated our being constantly amid the snow and ice.

3. At the end of May the ship began slowly to settle, and the water rose between the ice and the hull on the forepart of the ship. But we soon discovered, that

these small changes would not suffice to free us from our prison house, but that we must ourselves endeavour to loosen the fetters which held us fast, if it were only to banish gloomy thoughts of the future by action of some kind or other. Hence constant digging, sawing and blasting on our floe through May, June, July, and August —labours in which the whole crew of the ship, with the exception of the sick and of the cook, took part; labours, alas! which admonished us of the impotence of man when he contends against the power of Nature. Only on the port side of the ship were our efforts to dig through the floe at all successful; on the starboard side the floe had been so enormously increased by the tables of ice forced upon one another, that we had not pierced through the ice after sinking a shaft eighteen feet deep; and at last the water, forcing itself through the pores of the ice, compelled us to desist from the labour of sinking deeper. The process of sawing was possible only where we had broken through the ice—that is on the port side; yet even there the great thickness of the floe necessitated the construction of longer instruments, for which the iron casing of the engine-room had to furnish the material. The difficulty of sawing increases with the thickness of the ice in an almost incredible manner. It is easy enough to cut through a floe, four or five feet thick, but to break up one, eight or ten feet thick, is a matter of great difficulty. Our saws too, even when they were lengthened, permitted a play of only a foot; and their twisting, as they cut deep, proved a great hindrance. Besides, when we had cut to the depth of a fathom, the saws were always frozen fast, and when we attempted to free them by blasting they were very often broken in pieces. But even the sections, made with so much difficulty, often proved to be quite useless, as they were frozen together again by broken ice left in the cut. Blasting with gunpowder proved as ineffectual as in the previous year; in fact the process was only applicable to ice-blocks which had been loosened by sawing, and which could not be broken up by the crow-bar alone.

4. By the middle of June we were at last convinced that the thickness of the ice rendered it impossible to join together, by sawing, the two and-twenty holes which we had dug out round the ship. Henceforward our labours were confined to the formation of a basin at the forepart of the ship. Although we saw the impossibility of liberating the vessel, as long as she rested on a mountain of ice, we hoped that the basin would help to break up the floe, and that the *Tegetthoff* would of itself return to its normal position. The gliding down of the ship, raised as it was, to its natural water-line

might indeed easily end in a catastrophe, but we braved this peril when we thought of the vain attempts we had made to free her. Though the ship sunk so much in the course of the summer, that its height above the water-line was a little more than two feet in the fore part of the ship, and three feet in the after part, this circumstance in our favour was outweighed by the disadvantage of the rapid melting away of the ice at its sides. The ship, freed from its covering of ice, stood so high above it, that in order to guard against the danger of its overturning we were obliged, in the second half of the summer, to shore it up by strong timbers fastened to its masts. It looked no longer like a ship, but like a building ready to fall in! In the middle of July Lieutenant Weyprecht ordered Krisch, the engineer, to construct heavy chisels and borers to ascertain the thickness of the ice. After long and hard labour, we found that after boring through several ice-tables, to a depth of twenty-seven feet, we still struck on ice! Every attempt, therefore, to break through this accumulation had to be given up, and we contented ourselves with leading the basin we had formed on the fore part round the larboard side of the ship. On the 27th of the month, twenty tons of coal were removed to the ice, in order to lighten the ship as much as possible, and every day we had to look to the props which steadied the ship, as the melting of the ice rendered them unsafe. In the following weeks, the bows continued to sink into the water, while the after-part as a natural consequence was raised up.

5. Even in the month of July, the weather was generally gloomy and unsettled. We had several times two or three inches of snow, and the showers were mingled with mist, rain, and snow, as had been the case in June. The winds were generally from the west; the mean temperature of the month was $+1\cdot2°$ R.; on the 8th of July, the black bulb thermometer marked $+33\cdot7°$ R. and the temperature in the shade at the same date amounted to $+1°$ R. But neither wind nor temperature made any change in our position. The sun on which our liberation depended was seldom visible; and the winds on which we had counted failed to blow. For weeks we watched for the formation of fissures round the ship. Fissures indeed were formed, but at such a distance that they were utterly useless to us. On the 16th of June, one opened towards the south-east; but it was at least two miles distant, and in the middle of July it was only half a mile nearer to us. Nothing, absolutely nothing, was to be seen from the deck but ice, and Klotz, coming down one day from the

top-sail yard, described our position with a melancholy laconic brevity: "Nix als Eisch, und nix als Eisch und nit a bisserl a Wosser." (*Nothing but ice, ice everywhere, and not a patch of water.*) Amid such impressions all hope gradually left us. The drifting of the ice ceased to animate our hopes. Even the approach of a fissure on the 29th of July to the distance of three quarters of a mile, in consequence of heavy gales from the south and west, ended in miserable disappointment. A movement in the ice which began a little way off on the 6th of August, resulted only in the diminishing of our floe. There was no essential change in the remainder of this month, except that the monthly mean temperature fell to $+0·32°$ R. We had the greatest extreme of heat on the 4th of August, $+4·4°$ R.; but on the last day of the month we had $4·6°$ degrees of cold.

6. For some time we had been surprised by the appearance of a large dark mass of ice, the distance of which prevented us from making a closer acquaintance with it. Our life on the narrow space of our floe had quite assumed the character of that of mere insects, who dwell on the leaf of a tree and care not to know its edges. Excursions of one or two miles were regarded as displaying an extraordinary amount of the spirit of enterprise and discovery. On the 14th some of us

pushed on for about four miles to the group of ice just mentioned, and discovered it to be a very large iceberg. Two moraines lay on its broad back. These were the first stones and pieces of rock we had seen for a long time, and so great was our joy at these messengers of land, that we rummaged about among the heaps of rubbish, with as much zeal as if we had found ourselves among the treasures of India. Some of the party found what they fancied to be gold (pyrites), and gravely considered, whether they would be able to take a quantity of it back to Dalmatia. Although the glaciers of Novaya Zemlya could not shed icebergs of such magnitude as that on which we now stood, we all held it for certain that it had come from thence. Not one of us had the least presentiment that it could belong to new lands, to which at that time we were near. Even the other ice-bergs, which we discovered in increasing numbers on the following days, did not as yet speak to us the language of a message to fill us with hope and ardour. Our walk to the "dirt ice-berg" was an event in our monotonous life, and was often repeated. These expeditions enabled us also to form some conception of the size of our floe, the diameter of which could not be less than six or seven miles.

7. August 18—the birthday of his Majesty our Emperor, the ship was dressed with flags, the only form left to us of expressing our loyalty. Our dinner was as sumptuous as the circumstances permitted, though fasting would have been more appropriate, as the third day after this was the anniversary of that sad and gloomy day, on which we were inclosed in the ice. In order to visit an ice-berg which lay to the north-west of us, we ventured beyond our floe for the first time and passed over a fissure to some drifting ice-floes which lay in the way. A seal lying on the ice was immediately attacked by our dogs, but succeeded after many efforts in reaching its hole. From the top of the ice-berg, which was about 60 feet high, we discovered that the few openings in the ice were not navigable "leads" but isolated holes utterly unconnected, and therefore useless for navigation.

8. We had continually drifted, since the beginning of February, first to the north-west and then to the north, with few modifications; at that date, we had reached our greatest East Longitude, and winds appeared as before to be the main cause of this drifting. At the end of that month there was a succession of calms, and we lay almost motionless in latitude 79°, and longitude 71°. The subjoined table shows our change of place in the following months.

Time.	Latitude.	Longitude.	Time.	Latitude.	Longitude.
March 3, 1873	79° 13'	69° 32'	June 27, 1873	79° 13·7'	59° 46·0
,, 9 ,,	79 19	68 28	,, 28 ,,	79 15·5	59 35·4
,, 14 ,,	79 20	68 28	July 3 ,,	79 15·2	59 14·8
,, 20 ,,	79 33	68 52	,, 4 ,,	79 14·8	59 13·3
,, 25 ,,	79 23	67 17	,, 8 ,,	79 15·2	59 5·8
,, 27 ,,	79 15	67 29	,, 10 ,,	79 13·2	59 9·0
,, 29 ,,	79 14	67 35	,, 15 ,,	79 9·8	59 52·6
April 2 ,,	79 5	66 49	,, 18 ,,	79 7·3	59 50·4
,, 3 ,,	79 5	66 42	,, 19 ,,	79 7·6	59 35·1
,, 7 ,,	79 4	—	,, 20 ,,	79 8·7	59 33·6
,, 10 ,,	79 12	68 1	,, 21 ,,	79 9·2	59 33·1
,, 12 ,,	79 19	67 43	,, 22 ,,	79 9·0	59 34·1
,, 13 ,,	79 20	67 40	,, 33 ,,	79 6·6	59 34·2
,, 15 ,,	79 14	67 0	,, 24 ,,	79 7·1	59 29·5
,, 19 ,,	79 18	65 51	,, 25 ,,	79 6·6	59 27·3
,, 20 ,,	79 19	65 37	,, 31 ,,	78 58·5	60 25·5
,, 27 ,,	79 13·5	64 37·0	August 1 ,,	78 56·9	60 40·6
,, 28 ,,	79 12·2	64 41·8	,, 4 ,,	79 0·4	61 6·2
May 1 ,,	79 15·8	64 58·8	,, 13 ,,	79 25·4	61 6·6
, 2 ,,	79 17·1	65 3·9	,, 14 ,,	79 24·5	61 16·3
,, 6 ,,	79 16·0	65 0·5	,, 16 ,,	79 27·8	61 7·6
,, 10 ,,	79 20·4	65 41·9	,, 19 ,,	79 29·1	61 31·0
,, 11 ,,	79 20·2	65 32·4	,, 21 ,,	79 31·3	61 44·8
,, 13 ,,	79 19·7	65 15·8	,, 30 ,,	79 43·0	60 23·7
,, 14 ,,	79 19·8	64 45·6	,, 31 ,,	79 42·5	60 5·6
,, 16 ,,	79 15·5	63 39·0	Sept. 2 ,,	79 40·2	60 32·9
,, 17 ,,	79 13·1	63 21·7	,, 5 ,,	79 41·3	60 12·5
,, 22 ,,	79 9·2	62 3·5	,, 8 ,,	79 34·2	59 47·3
,, 29 ,,	79 2·4	62 55·5	,, 9 ,,	79 33·6	59 45·9
,, 30 ,,	79 2·5	62 54·2	,, 10 ,,	79 32·2	59 53·1
,, 31 ,,	79 2·5	62 53·9	,, 16 ,,	79 45·6	61 30·5
June 1 ,,	79 2·4	62 43·2	,, 23 ,,	79 49·6	61 58·1
,, 3 ,,	79 0·4	62 29·7	,, 30 ,,	79 58·3	60 41·1
,, 5 ,,	79 1·3	62 24·8	Oct. 16 ,,	79 54·6	60 34·7
,, 6 ,,	79 1·1	62 20·2	,, 19 ,,	79 53·9	60 40·6
,, 9 ,,	79 5·4	61 31·4	,, 23 ,,	79 44·5	60 7·9
,, 10 ,,	79 5·3	61 23·6	,, 26 ,,	79 44·3	59 17·1
,, 11 ,,	79 4·3	61 21·3	,, 27 ,,	79 44·0	59 14·1
,, 18 ,,	79 6·6	61 5·2	,, 28 ,,	79 43·8	59 6·6
,, 20 ,,	79 8·6	61 2·8	,, 29 ,,	79 44·8	59 9·8
,, 22 ,,	79 9·2	60 54·9	,, 30 ,,	79 49·0	58 59·9
,, 24 ,,	79 8·4	60 31·8	,, 31 ,,	79 50·6	58 53·7
,, 25 ,,	79 11·2	60 14·6	Ship		
,, 26 ,,	79 13·3	59 55·3	Land ice	79 51·1	58 56·0

9. The meteorological observations of the expedition, and the course of the *Tegetthoff*, have been ably analysed

by Vice-Admiral Baron von Wüllerstorff-Urbair in the *Mittheilungen* of the Imperial Academy of Sciences of Vienna, and while I refer the curious reader to these reports for a fuller discussion of these questions, I subjoin the most important paragraphs of the Admiral's report which concern the course of the *Tegetthoff*.

"Under ordinary circumstances a ship drifts on with the floe; it is imprisoned and necessarily obeys the force of the wind and the sea-currents. Its course, consequently, corresponds to the combined effect of these forces. But, inasmuch as the *Tegetthoff* was not in the free sea, but was driven along for the greater part of the time in close pack ice, the ship not only obeyed the general movement of the ice, which was dependent on the direction of the winds and currents of the sea, but was also influenced by its vicinity to coasts and by the greater or lesser accumulation of ice.

"In so far as the *Tegetthoff* with her hull and masts presented a greater surface to the wind, the floe, on which it was imprisoned, would necessarily receive an excess of movement in the direction of the wind. If this excess formed an angle with the direction of the movement of the ice, the ship's floe would deviate to the side of the least resistance, and drift according to the resultant between wind and resistance. Thus it might be that the ship's course deviated from the wind, even in a direction opposed to it. But these anomalies certainly were not great, and could not well be estimated, because the deviations which thus arose depended on the direction of the wind, on the density and mass of the ice, on causes, in fact, which could not be exhibited under numerical relations.

" If we compare the statements, as given in the *Meteorological Journal*,[1] concerning the ice-drift and ice-pressures, it is seen that the maximum of both occurred in those parts of the sea in which the ship was within the action of the ice coming from the Sea of Kara, and that the greatest deviations in the ship's course necessarily happened there.

" With respect to another abnormal deviation in the ship's course, it cannot be doubted that this depended on the vicinity of Franz Josef Land, towards which the masses of ice drifted under the action of continuous south-west winds; and were again driven back, thus forming a circle in their movement. It would seem natural to assume the existence of a sea-current in order to explain this peculiarity; but the configuration of that land and its coasts, or the greater or lesser amount of immovable ice, or, lastly, the prevailing winds in those regions may have influenced the direction of the movement of the ice, and consequently of the ship's course.

[1] See Appendix.

"If we consider the prevalence of winds, as furnished by Weyprecht's observations for more than two years, we find south-west winds prevailing in the southern part of the seas that were navigated, and north-east winds in the northern part of those seas.

"If the sea to the east of Franz Josef Land should not be broken by larger groups of islands, or by masses of land, but be a vast range of ocean, the winds would be free from the influence of land, and blow in a north-easterly direction, and exhibit, so to speak, the phenomenon of a Polar north-east trade wind. If it should be the case, that north-east winds prevail to the north of the 78th or 79th degree of north latitude, and, at the same time, south-west winds to the south of that same degree, the notion of a sea-current must be dismissed, and a revolving movement in the ice assumed, in the opposite direction to the hands of a clock. The observations of Weyprecht on these winds establish their circulatory character. The curve of deviation in the course of the *Tegetthoff* seems to be in harmony with this assumption. But these suppositions cannot be accepted, until observations be made on the winds to the south of 79° N. L. at the same season of the year with those which were so successfully made by Weyprecht to the north of this degree.

"The following arguments, however, would seem to

favour the supposition of the existence of a sea-current. The curve at the commencement of its deviation corresponds pretty nearly with the direction which the Gulf Stream would take after passing round Norway, and in its further course with that current, which comes out of the Sea of Kara between Novaya Zemlya and Cape Taimyr, and which undoubtedly exists, though its course has to be more accurately determined.

"However small may be the value we assign to the winds in explanation of the deviation in the *Tegetthoff's* course, it is at any rate impossible to ascribe those phenomena to the influence of the coast formation. We must, therefore, assume either, that the different directions of the wind produce a constant circulation of the ice in the sea to the north of 79°; or that currents known to exist in this and contiguous seas cannot be excluded from the small part of the ocean lying between Novaya Zemlya and Franz Josef Land."

From these and other grounds the Vice-Admiral Baron von Wüllersdorf draws the following conclusions:—

"It is probable that there exists a sea-current in the seas between Novaya Zemlya and Franz Josef Land; that at any rate, its existence cannot positively be denied, although the prevailing winds may produce similar phenomena.

"That there is a great probability that the Ocean stretches far to the north and east beyond the eastern end of Novaya Zemlya."

10. During the summer Orel took soundings of the depth of the sea, which he was prevented from continuing in the winter by the frost. These show its shallowness on the north of Novaya Zemlya, especially towards Franz Josef Land. A bank, over

SOUNDING IN THE FROZEN OCEAN.

which we drifted in the summer of 1873, and which we explored with a drag-net, was the principal source of the collection of marine fauna, which we shall speak of in a later chapter. These soundings also enabled Orel to prove the small increase of the temperature of the sea at any considerable depth. He used in his experiments the maximum and minimum thermometer of Casella. The specimens we collected showed, that the bottom of the sea consists of layers of mud and shells. The soundings are exhibited in the following table:—

Time.	Metres.	Time.	Metres.	Time.	Metres.
July 20, 1872	400	June 19, 1873	186	Aug. 9, 1873	244
„ 28 „	115	„ 20 „	220	„ 10 „	225
„ 31 „	250	„ 21 „	195	„ 11 „	209
Aug. 3 „	130	„ 22 „	200	„ 12 „	214
„ 4 „	80	„ 23 „	169	„ 13 „	189
„ 22 „	36	„ 24 „	178	„ 14 „	177
„ 30 „	170	„ 25 „	195	„ 15 „	170
Sept. 16 „	100	„ 26 „	220	„ 16 „	170
„ 25 „	90	„ 27 „	227	„ 17 „	174
„ 29 „	85	„ 28 „	233	„ 18 „	148
„ 30 „	190	„ 29 „	240	„ 19 „	152
Oct. 2 „	170	„ 30 „	240	„ 20 „	138
„ 9 „	450	July 1 „	240	„ 21 „	130
Nov. 14 „	345	„ 3 „	245	„ 22 „	131
Jan. 28, 1873	510	„ 4 „	250	„ 23 „	128
Mar. 27 „	450	„ 5 „	235	„ 24 „	145
April 28 „	350	„ 6 „	235	„ 25 „	140
May 17 „	230	„ 7 „	274	„ 26 „	185
„ 18 „	187	„ 8 „	266	„ 27 „	219
„ 19 „	172	„ 9 „	250	„ 28 „	180
„ 20 „	163	„ 10 „	250	„ 29 „	132
„ 21 „	138	„ 11 „	236	„ 30 „	211
„ 22 „	186	„ 12 „	265	„ 31 „	197
„ 23 „	162	„ 13 „	247	Sept. 1 „	260
„ 25 „	177	„ 14 „	215	„ 2 „	142
„ 25 „	182	„ 15 „	195	„ 3 „	212
„ 26 „	186	„ 16 „	184	„ 4 „	215
„ 27 „	249	„ 17 „	200	„ 5 „	178
„ 28 „	251	„ 18 „	240	„ 6 „	168
„ 29 „	254	„ 19 „	232	„ 7 „	204
„ 30 „	253	„ 20 „	231	„ 8 „	250
„ 31 „	256	„ 21 „	231	„ 9 „	240
June 1 „	238	„ 22 „	226	„ 10 „	218
„ 2 „	210	„ 23 „	198	„ 11 „	168
„ 3 „	183	„ 24 „	205	„ 12 „	127
„ 4 „	207	„ 25 „	216	„ 13 „	132
„ 5 „	200	„ 26 „	218	„ 14 „	137
„ 6 „	198	„ 27 „	218	„ 15 „	111
„ 7 „	190	„ 28 „	256	„ 16 „	134
„ 8 „	215	„ 29 „	260	„ 17 „	178
„ 9 „	231	„ 30 „	236	„ 18 „	175
„ 10 „	203	„ 31 „	234	„ 19 „	275
„ 11 „	240	Aug. 1 „	225	„ 20 „	300
„ 12 „	218	„ 2 „	219	„ 21 „	220
„ 13 „	211	„ 3 „	173	„ 22 „	168
„ 14 „	235	„ 4 „	188	„ 24 „	237
„ 15 „	161	„ 5 „	210	„ 25 „	325
„ 16 „	184	„ 6 „	107	Oct. 28 „	165
„ 17 „	222	„ 7 „	216	„ 31 „	210
„ 18 „	200	„ 8 „	184		

CHAPTER XI.

NEW LANDS.

1. We spent the latter half of August in seal-hunting, for it was only by the use of fresh meat, that we were able to contend with, if not prevent, cases of scurvy. Day after day lines of hunters lay in wait before the fissures at the edge of our floe, and in the evening our dogs generally had to drag in the sledges several seals to the ship. Many of these creatures which we wounded sank and disappeared. All these seals belonged to the class Phoca Groenlandica. Walruses were never to be seen, and once only in an "ice-hole" we came across a shoal of White whales, which however seemed to be moving on. In the capture of seals we sometimes used a light boat, made of water-proof sail-cloth, which two men could easily drag out of the water. Some of our people too had learnt the use of the harpoon. By the end of September, we had killed in one way or another some 40 seals, and as we shot many of the birds

which flew round us, and on an average one bear a week, we were seldom without fresh meat. With the exception of Krisch, the engineer, who suffered from lung disease, and of the carpenter, who had become lame from a scorbutic contraction of the joints, all on the sick list recovered under the influence of work in the open air and of the improved diet.

2. The covering of deep soft snow, which had been so troublesome, almost disappeared at the beginning of autumn, and the surface of the ice had been transformed by evaporation into a firm mass like the congealed snow of a glacier, so that we were able to walk on its hard surface without sinking; only the numerous small ice-lakes, on the floes, impeded our excursions. In all these signs, we were reminded of the near approach of winter, and it seemed that, drifting as we were constantly towards the north we should spend it nearer to the pole than any other expedition had ever done. On the 25th the sun set at midnight. The period intervening between this and the time when the sun ceases to reappear, may be regarded as the autumn of the Arctic region. For some time the light had so diminished, that our quarters again became dark at night, and from the 19th of July we were obliged to use a light in order to read at midnight. On the 29th of August after falls of rain

and snow succeeded by north winds, the ship was stiffened in a coating of ice. The rigging was covered with an incrustation of ice of an inch thick, and pieces of ice of a pound weight sometimes fell on the deck, rendering walking on it neither comfortable nor safe. After a succession of frosts and thaws, complete congelation at last set in, and when the moon was up, the masts and rigging shone like burnished silver.

3. The second summer was gone. It had come in with the hope and promise of liberation, and patiently had we awaited this result. With sad resignation we now looked forward to another winter. But once more it was to be seen in our case, how great is the power of men to endure dangers and hardships, when these come upon them not suddenly but gradually. A few months ago, the thought that we should be prisoners on the ice, bound to our floe, for a second winter, would have been unendurable. But now that the intolerable thought had become a stern fact, we accepted and endured it. But often as we went on deck and cast our eyes over the wastes, from which there was no escape, the despairing thought recurred, that next year we should have to return home—without having achieved anything, or at most with a narrative of a long drift in the ice. Not a man among us believed in the possibility

of discoveries, though discoveries beyond our utmost hopes lay immediately before us.

4. A memorable day was the 30th August 1873 in 79° 43′ Lat. and 59° 33′ E. Long. That day brought a surprise, such as only the awakening to a new life can produce. About mid-day, as we were leaning on the bulwarks of the ship and scanning the gliding mists, through which the rays of the sun broke ever and anon, a wall of mist, lifting itself up suddenly, revealed to us afar off in the north-west, the outlines of bold rocks, which in a few minutes seemed to grow into a radiant Alpine land! At first we all stood transfixed and hardly believing what we saw. Then carried away by the reality of our good fortune we burst forth into shouts of joy :—" Land, Land, Land at last ! " There was now not a sick man on board the *Tegetthoff*. The news of the discovery spread in an instant. Every one rushed on deck, to convince himself with his own eyes, that the expedition was not after all a failure—there before us lay the prize that could not be snatched from us. Yet not by our own action, but through the happy caprice of our floe and as in a dream had we won it, but when we thought of the floe, drifting without intermission, we felt with redoubled pain, that we were at the mercy of its movements. As yet we had secured no winter harbour, from which the exploration of the

strange land could be successfully undertaken. For the present, too, it was not within the verge of possibility to reach and visit it. If we had left our floe, we should have been cut off and lost. It was only under the influence of the first excitement that we made a rush over our ice field, although we knew that numberless fissures made it impossible to reach the land. But, difficulties notwithstanding, when we ran to the edge of our floe, we beheld from a ridge of ice the mountains and glaciers of the mysterious land. Its valleys seemed to our fond imagination clothed with green pastures, over which herds of rein-deer roamed in undisturbed enjoyment of their liberty, and far from all foes.

5. For thousands of years this land had lain buried from the knowledge of men, and now its discovery had fallen into the lap of a small band, themselves almost lost to the world, who far from their home remembered the homage due to their sovereign and gave to the newly-discovered territory the name

KAISER FRANZ-JOSEF'S LAND.

With loud hurrahs we drank to the health of our Emperor in grog hastily made on deck in an iron coffee-pot, and then dressed the *Tegetthoff* with flags. All cares, for the present at least, disappeared, and with them the passive monotony of our lives. There was not a day, there was hardly an hour, in which this mysterious land did not henceforth occupy our thoughts and attention. We discussed whether this or that elevation in the grey and misty distance were a mountain, or an island, or a glacier. All our attempts to solve the question of the extent of the land lying before us were of course still more fruitless. From the head-land which we had first seen (Cape Tegetthoff), to its hazy outline in the northeast, it seemed to extend nearly a degree; but as even its southernmost parts were at a great distance from us, it was impossible to arrive at anything more definite than a mere approximation to its configuration. The size and number of the ice-bergs which we had recently fallen in with were now amply explained,—they were indisputable witnesses of its great extent and its vast glaciation.

6. At the end of August and the beginning of September north winds drove us somewhat towards the south, so that the outlines of the land were still more faintly defined. But at the end of September we were again driven towards the north-west and reached 79° 58' the highest degree of latitude to which the *Tegetthoff* and its floe drifted. We now saw an island at some distance off—afterwards called Hochstetter island— lying before us. Its rocky outlines were distinctly visible,

and the opportunity of *reaching the land by a forced march* seemed more favourable than any which had been presented. It might also be the last chance offered to us, for our fears lest we might drift out of sight of this land were well founded. Six of her crew now left the *Tegetthoff* and committed themselves to the destiny, which the movement of the ice had in store for them. The east winds, which had prevailed during the last days, had forced the ice landward and the pressures had crushed in the edges of our floe, and greatly diminished its size. We rushed over the grinding, groaning, broken walls of drifting ice and so great was our ardour, that we took no notice, when some one or other of the party tripped and fell. Each panted to reach the land. We had already gone half way, the ship having long disappeared from our eyes, when there arose a mist which enveloped everything, so that the masses of ice looked like high mountains through the hazy atmosphere. Of the land itself we could see nothing, and no choice was left to us but to return to the ship through the mist. The compass was little help, and within the barriers of recently broken ice the traces of our steps were lost. We took at last a wrong direction and were following it up, in spite of Jubinal's loud barks to divert us. As he ran backwards and forwards, magnified in the mist he ran many risks of being mistaken for a bear. What the sagacity of six men could not do, this the instinct of the animal effected. Exhausted by our own exertions we yielded ourselves to his guidance and he actually brought us into the right track—and back to the ship.

CHAPTER XII.

THE AUTUMN OF 1873.—*THE STRANGE LAND VISITED.*

1. THE autumn was unusually mild, though stormy and gloomy. The thermometer up to the 20th of September fell daily some degrees below zero (R.), and occasionally we had rain. At the end of the month the minimum temperature ranged from $-8°$ to $-12°$ R., and the mean temperature of the month was as low as $-3\cdot3°$ R. The mildness of the season was, perhaps, connected with the unusual recession of the ice-barrier in the south; though it might have been a consequence of the open water which had been formed under the land during the drifting of the floes. The land itself was but seldom visible, and heavy masses of dark blue clouds, which are peculiar to southern latitudes, generally hung over it. Frequent falls of snow again covered everything around us. Parhelia were sometimes visible, and these were generally the precursors of driving snow, which reared deep drifts round the ship. The numerous little

lakes on the ice-floes were frozen over in the night even in the earlier part of August, and at the end of the month these bore us during the day. The clear mirror of their surface cracked whenever the temperature fell suddenly some degrees, while the effect of contraction in the ship was followed by the noises which we called "Schüsse." The "ice-holes" were overspread with a viscous ropy ice, which was strong enough to bear us at their edges. The ship now stood out from the ice; her hull was about fourteen feet above the surrounding surface of snow. To facilitate egress and ingress, we constructed steps of ice on each side of the vessel. After the 7th of September our efforts to free the ship were given up. The little basin at the forepart of the ship—the result of the toil of many months—was completely frozen over, and afforded us the recreation of skating as a reward for our labours.

2. The experience of the past greatly strengthened all the grounds and motives which so readily presented themselves to abandon our helpless vessel in the following summer and attempt the return to Europe by means of sledges and boats. If there had been no other reason for this resolution, regard for our health would have dictated the step. Our supply of lemon-juice was so reduced, as to leave scarcely a doubt as to the necessity

of attempting to return. But amid these prudential considerations, we were filled with fear lest we should be unable to explore the mysterious land we had discovered.

3. The daylight now began to fail. On the 9th of September the sun set at 8.30 and the stars were visible at night. About the middle of the month lamps were kept burning all the night through in our quarters below, and our environment, never very animated, again wore the aspect of the dark realm of ice. The visits of birds became rarer, although they did not quite leave us, as long as there was any open water near. The divers and auks had already disappeared. They flew in long lines southward, and as they whizzed past us through the rigging of the ship, we acknowledged the superiority of these little creatures to us and to our ship, which was never to hoist its sails again. The ice birds, and the robber gulls, still remained with us. We once shot a rose-coloured gull (Ross's gull), said to belong only to North America and Iceland. On the 28th we saw the last snow bunting. The first aurora was seen on the 22nd, and during the winter its light fell not merely on the Frozen Ocean but on the distant Franz-Josef's land, showing us that we were not drifting away from it. By the end of the month we had drifted to the eightieth degree of latitude, nearly ; and every cliff of the land, even the most insignificant,

emerging at a distance from the ice, had charms enough to call us all on deck.

4. In the second half of October, winds from the north and north-east had driven us towards the south and south-west, and as we neared the land we saw that the ice-fields were broken up by their contact with its immovable barrier. Our own floe had been greatly diminished from the general pressure of the ice. On the 1st of October we were driven so near the land that we found ourselves in the midst of the destruction going on in the ice. Our ice-floe was shattered and broken, and so rapidly had it diminished in size, that the distance of the ship from the edge of the floe, which was 1,300 paces on the 1st, amounted to only 875 two days afterwards. On the 6th it had diminished to 200 paces, so that it was reduced to a mere fragment of its former size. The shocks it now received, caused the ship to quiver and shake, and we heard the cracking and straining in its timbers, which kept us on the tenter-hook of expectation lest the ice should suddenly break up. It seemed as if we were doomed to a repetition of the trials and dangers of the preceding winter. The bags of necessaries to be taken with us if we should be forced to leave the ship, were kept in readiness for immediate use. As we watched the advancing wall of ice, and heard the too well-

known howl it sent forth, and saw how fissures were formed at the edge of the floe, the days of the ice-pressures were painfully recalled, and the thought constantly returned—what will be the end of all this? The land we had so longed to visit lay indeed before us, but the very sight of it had become a torment; it seemed to be as unattainable as before; and, if our ship should reach it, it appeared too likely that it would be as a wreck on its inhospitable shore. Many were the plans we formed and debated, but all were alike impracticable, and all owed their existence to the wish to escape from the destruction that stared us in the face. Such were our outlooks when on the 31st of October we were driven close to a headland of no great height, about three miles distant from the ship, and found ourselves in the midst of ice-bergs, several of which were of considerable magnitude. Towards this, the bergs, or we ourselves, or both, were rapidly drifting, as the soundings showed. If the icebergs drifted, they would of course crush all the ice-fields which stood in their way. We were now in 79° 51′ N.L. and 58° 56′ E. Long. Here exactly in the longitude of Admiralty peninsula of Novaya Zemlya, and with the ship lying north and south, we were to pass the winter—but harbourless.

5. On the forenoon of the 1st of November, the land

lay to the north-west of us in the twilight. The lines of rocks were so clearly and distinctly seen, that we were convinced that it could be reached without endangering our return to the ship. There was no room for hesitation; full of energy and wild excitement, we clambered over the ice-walls lying to the northward, which consisted of barriers, fifty feet high, of huge pieces of ice recently forced up amid the pressure. These passed, we came on a broad surface of young ice, which showed that there had been open water there a short time before. Over the surface of this young ice we now ran towards the land. We crossed the ice-foot and actually stepped on it. Snow and rocks and broken ice surrounded us on every side; a land more desolate could not be found on earth than the island we walked on; all this we saw not. To us it was a paradise; and this paradise we called Wilczek Island.

6. So great was our joy at having reached the Land at last, that we bestowed on all we saw an attention which, in itself, it in no way merited. We looked into every rent in the rocks, we touched every block, we were ravished with the varied forms and outlines which each crevice presented. We talked in grand style of the frozen slopes of its hollows as glaciers! Nothing was of greater moment in these first hours than the question of

its geological character, and great was our surprise to find here the same rocks, with which we had become acquainted at the Pendulum Islands during the second German North Polar Expedition. The columnar conformation of these Dolerite rocks singularly resembled those of Griper Roads and Shannon Island. The vegetation was indescribably meagre and miserable, consisting merely of a few lichens. The drift-wood we expected to find was nowhere to be seen. We looked for traces of the rein-deer and the fox, but our search was utterly fruitless. The Land appeared to be without a single living creature. We then ascended a rocky height on the southern margin of the island, whence we had a view of the frozen ocean extending some miles beyond the ship. There was something sublime to the imagination in the utter loneliness of a land never before visited; felt all the more from the extraordinary character of our position. We had become exceedingly sensitive to new impressions, and a golden mist which rose on the southern horizon of an invisible ice-hole, and which spread itself, like an undulating curtain, before the glow of the noontide heavens had to us the charm of a landscape in Ceylon.

7. How vexatious was it to feel, that if we had reached this Land some weeks earlier, we might have explored it without the risk of being cut off from the ship. For

some days the sun had sunk below the horizon, and the twilight of noon admitted of only a few short excursions from the ship, quite insufficient to satisfy our earnest desire to learn more of its structure and configuration; and we much feared lest the constant north winds should cause us to drift out of sight of it. Southwards stretched a flat surface of bluish-grey ice, and beyond the distant ship, a large "ice-hole" from whose yellow mirror there arose undulating mists. Beyond this again stretched dark lines of floes running parallel to the horizon, over which, in the south, hung the sky in deep carmine. We scrambled over a rugged slope covered with ice as smooth as glass, which ran into the interior of the little island, in order to get a clear view northward; but we were compelled to return without achieving our purpose, for we feared to absent ourselves longer from the ship. We accordingly went back but returned next day to explore. But these barren days and small events made a profound impression on our minds, and even Carlsen, the old and tried navigator of the frozen deep, wore on his breast, beneath his fur coat, the star of the order of St. Olaf, to do due honour to the dignity of discovery. We built a pyramid of stones six feet high on the island, and fixed in it one of our flags attached to a pole.

8. On the 3rd of November a party of us started about

eight o'clock in the morning, when it was quite dark, to attempt to reach a glacier which we had seen, on the north of the island and on the other side of a frozen inlet of the sea. We took with us a small sledge drawn by three dogs, and, in constant fear of being cut off from

APPROACHING THE LAND BY MOONLIGHT.

the ship, we pressed on over a level surface of snow towards some objects suffused with a dim rosy light, which seemed to float over them. As we neared them we found them to be ice-bergs which sparkled like jewels, and which we took to be the terminal precipice of the glacier we were in search of. It was only, however, after some hours that we came actually in sight of it ; the ship having meanwhile disappeared from our view. Suddenly there emerged before us, in the east, a white band, which proved to be the terminal front of the glacier, which, as we approached it, we were surprised to find had an inclination of only two or three degrees. Its highest point, therefore, must have been at a very great distance. On its left side there was a moraine of great depth. When we began our return to the ship, the rosy evening light had disappeared from the higher clouds, while it became clearer behind the gigantic mass of the glacier, so that its dark outline stood out strongly marked on the heavens. It was quite dark when we again drew near the ship, but the brave Carlsen, armed with rifle and walrus-lance for any emergency came out to meet us.

9. In an excursion on the 6th of November we reached a point on the north-west of Wilczek Island—passing for the first time during this expedition beyond the eightieth degree of north latitude—whence we could see the mainland of the new country stretching before us under the silver light of the moon. An indescribable loneliness lay on its snowy mountains, faintly illuminated by the span of twilight in the south and by the light of the moon. If the ice on the shore, as it was moved by the ebb and flow of the tide, had not sent forth shrill notes, and had not the wind sighed, as it passed over the edges of the rocks, the stillness of death would have lain on the pale and spectral landscape. We hear of the

solemn silence of the forest or of the desert, or of a city buried in sleep during the night ; but what is this silence to the silence of a land with its cold glacier mountains losing themselves in snows and mists which can never be explored, and the very existence of which had remained unknown from creation till this moment ?

10. On the 7th another short expedition towards the south-west of Wilczek Island, was carried out ; but notwithstanding all our exertions we were unable to determine its configuration, even of the parts immediately contiguous to us. Until the spring of the following year, the whole island, except perhaps a portion of its southern side, remained a mystery to us.

CHAPTER XIII.

OUR SECOND WINTER IN THE ICE.

1. THE Land had meantime been thickly enveloped in its pure white mantle, and wreaths of snowdrifts lay over the rocks scattered over its surface. The light became fainter. Sometimes the precipitous faces of the glaciers seemed to glow in subdued rose colour through the leaden grey of the atmosphere. When new "ice-holes" appeared, a frosty vapour rose and spread over the surface of the ice; the ship and surrounding objects were covered as if with down; even the dogs were frosted white. We used to stand on deck and gaze on the sun as it sank, surrounded by the evening clouds, behind the jagged edges of the hummocks. Raised by refraction, he appeared for the last time on the 22nd of October with half his disc above the horizon, and the whole southern sky was for a time like a sea of fire over the cold, still forms and lines of ice. At length the disc disappeared, and masses of dark clouds moved up and obscured the

light still lingering in the sky. The long reign of night
began, and the wastes around us relapsed into the stern
sway of winter. A pale twilight still lingered for
some time, but its faint arc became smaller and feebler.
No shadows accompanied the forms of those who strayed
over the ice. The wind moaned in the frozen desert.
The darkness and the cold continually increased, till the
dome of night vaulted the lonely spot which had become
our home.

2. But the hope and expectation of successes to be
achieved, and the feeling that our safety was not immediately threatened, rendered this second winter a
happy contrast to the preceding one. We had now leisure
and calmness for intellectual occupations, which were,
indeed, the only means of relieving the monotony of
the long period of darkness. We lived like hermits
in our little cabins in the after-part of the ship, and
learned, that mental activity without any other joy,
suffices to make men happy and contented. The oppressive feeling of having to return ingloriously home,
which had always been disagreeably present to our
minds during the first winter, was no longer felt. We
had now a hope, the charms of which grew day by day,
that in the spring we should be able to leave the ship
and start on expeditions to explore the land we had discovered. Happy in this expectation, we could enjoy

the indescribable pleasures of good books, all the more that we were far from the busy haunts of men, and that the presence of danger clears and sharpens the understanding. Nowhere can a book be so valued as in such an isolated position as ours was. Great, therefore, was the advantage we possessed in a good library, consisting of books of science, and of the classics of literature. In fact, freed from the constantly recurring perils, which had been our portion in the first long Arctic night, this second winter was to all who actively employed their minds, comparatively a state of happiness, undisturbed by cares. With regard to the crew, they were kept in good humour by the increase of their comforts. As we had not the prospect of a third winter in the ice—which would have rendered a greater economy of our provisions imperative—we were enabled to provide them with a more generous diet.

3. In the last three weeks of November we had complete darkness, the sky clouded over and the weather bad. So dark was it, that our environment, though it was overspread with countless hummocks and ice-cliffs, looked like one black unbroken level. On the 31st of October most of the stars were visible about 3 o'clock in the afternoon; by 4 o'clock actual night prevailed. On the 16th of November large print was barely legible even at noon. On the 18th of the month

DEPARTURE OF THE SUN IN THE SECOND WINTER.

we were able to read the larger letters on the title-page of Vogt's *Geology* at the distance of a foot. At noon, on the 13th of December, not a letter of this same title-page was legible, even in clear weather. On the 5th of November there was a total eclipse of the moon, which then sank below the horizon and did not return till the 29th of that month. Its beams then fell on a large ice-hole, which had formed itself twenty miles to the south of the ship, which made us apprehensive, lest our floe should be driven by the north winds in a southerly direction. On the 4th of December the moon reached its highest declination, but, as it waned, it was constantly obscured by bad weather. I had reckoned on the return of moonlight to make an excursion of some days to the mainland. But the fickleness of the weather at the beginning of December compelled me to confine my wanderings to Wilczek Island, which I frequently visited, although with a thermometer at − 30° R. I was exposed to frost-bites in the face and hands, whenever I attempted to draw by the light of a lamp, and with only the protection of light woollen gloves.[1]

4. We observed during this winter, that, on the clearest nights, snow of the finest texture continued to fall, so

---

[1] I take this opportunity of stating that the originals of nearly all the illustrations of this book were drawn on the spot from nature, and that they have been reproduced as they were drawn.

that we saw the heavenly bodies, as it were, through a veil of fine gauze. In the moonlight this fine snow sparkled faintly, and its presence could only be discovered by a prickling on the skin. The constancy of these downfalls added of course to the depth of the snow under which the *Tegetthoff* was almost buried; indeed at the beginning of the spring she no longer stood out from the covering of snow, although her forepart was eleven-and-three-quarter feet, and her afterpart four-and-a-half feet, above the ice on which she rested. The air was also often filled with an indescribable quantity of driving snow; and when the wind dropped and permitted it to fall, we were struck with the profound stillness of our environment. The cold constantly increased and penetrated all the parts of the interior of the ship which were not artificially heated,[1] and almost all the fluids, which were not specially protected, were frozen. The various kinds of spirits on board were exposed on the 23rd of November to the cold at $-26°$ R.; at the end of an hour-and-a-half they still remained fluid. When the temperature fell to -28 R., hollands, common gin and maraschino were congealed in two-hours-and-a-half, but rum and brandy remained unchanged. On another occasion a mixture

[1] On the 24th of November the thermometer marked $-8°$ R. in the ship's hold. The screw propeller had been fast frozen a month before.

of two parts of pure alcohol to one part of water froze at $-35°$ R., cognac at $-38°$ R. This low temperature had so increased the thickness of the ice, that the basin of open water, which had been sawed through in the previous summer, was covered on the 3rd of January with ice three-and-a-half, and on the 20th with ice six-and-a-half feet thick.

5. On the 21st of December, the middle of the second long polar night—which lasted in all 125 days—was reached; and although we knew where the south lay, every trace of twilight had disappeared, and for six weeks we were enveloped in unbroken darkness. The figure of a man could not be discerned at a very short distance. In order to be able to sketch the ship, I had to illuminate it by torches. Those who made expeditions afoot were struck, as it were, with blindness. If they approached what seemed to be a lofty chain of mountains, over the ridge of which the planet Jupiter hung like a glowing point, they came at once on a dark wall of ice; and when they ascended the apparently far distant ridge, the planet stood almost in the zenith. There was something approaching to twilight only, when the crescent moon shone in her first quarter. On the 7th of December the sun was $12°$, and on the 21st $14\frac{1}{2}°$, below the horizon. We should not have seen the sun, could we have ascended the pinnacle of the Alps, which Pliny

imagined to be 120,000 feet high, or even from that summit of the Caucasus which Aristotle reckoned at 230,000 feet.

6. Distrusting the quiescent state of the ice, we had again stretched a tent over one half of the ship's deck, while the other portion was covered with snow trodden down as hard as a skating rink. The space for free movement was narrowed still further by the long boat placed between the two masts, by the stores of provisions kept in readiness for the possible disaster which might compel us to leave the ship, by the stand of rifles, by dog-kennels, and other inevitable impediments. In bad weather the dogs sheltered themselves under the tent, and sometimes showed ill-temper if their feet were trod on. There were places on deck where only their particular friends were safe from being bitten; Sumbu especially had a bad habit of lying behind a cask and springing out on every one that passed by. Here under its friendly shelter the men waited the summons to their meals. Hither came Carlsen to enjoy the opportunity of talking Norwegian with some one or other. The deck light shone feebly on all this, shedding its rays on the fine snow which fell through the tent roof. In the second half of the winter, when the deck was less frequented, the lantern became like the crew—more sleepy; and its dull light fell on hard-frozen sailcloth,

boards covered with snow, and on empty tin cases. Here, too, walked, of course, the deck-watch, enveloped in clothes from head to foot, with only their eyes uncovered, looking more like moving figures than men. The deck-watch had also to keep open the water-hole in the ice, to look out for bears, and to assist in reading off the thermometers exposed on the ice. They were on duty for two hours, and the moment they were relieved, they shot down into their quarters, as quickly as a harpooned whale dives under the waves. He, too whose duty it was to fetch the snow to be converted into water, was often to be seen on deck. Although the store of snow in which we lived was inexhaustible, yet, in order to be exempt from this duty in bad weather, it was the practice of those who were told off for this service to lay up a supply of blocks of frozen snow under the tent. Some of the crew showed the scrupulosity of chemists in their work. Before they proceeded to build up their pile, they brought specimens to the cook, in order to learn his opinion as to the residuum of salt in the ice.

7. With December a new era began for the dogs. A large snow house was built for them outside the ship, in which were placed their kennels, well filled with straw. The name of each dog was written on his house. And here let me remark, that the winter quarters

of the dogs should always be on the ice. To keep them under the deck-tent is unhealthy and inconvenient, and would be an impossibility if their numbers were great. Every morning Haller opened the door of the snow house, and out rushed the dogs, with their tails in the air, to begin forthwith a general fight. No shouts, no blows, not even the discharge of a rifle could separate the combatants. Pouring water over them at a temperature of $-30°$ R., though a somewhat barbarous way of producing peace, was successful only with the younger dogs. When the fight was over, the next object was to find out their special patron and the instant they recognised him they rushed upon him, tugged at his clothes, and thrust their noses inquiringly into his pockets. Each then made his morning round, visiting the places where he had hid in the snow a piece of bread or covered up a bit of seal. When they had satisfied their appetite, it was curious to observe how they would make it smooth over the hole in which they deposited their treasure, all the time cunningly turning their eyes right and left to see whether they were observed.

8. Their violence and eagerness having somewhat abated, we may observe the members of our pack one by one. The red giant there, who offers his paw as huge as a bear's, is named after a god of the heathen days of Lapland, "Jubinal;" and not a few legends surrounded

the accounts of his early life. A Siberian Israelite, so it was said, brought him from the north of Asia over the Ural. He was the victor in all fights, the leader of the sledge team, and could drag four men on a hard level path without any effort. The day before we sailed from Bremerhaven he tore a sheep to pieces. Every summer when he changed his coat, the sailors clad him in a canvas dress. Bop was his inferior in

TEKEL, SUMBU, AND JUDINAL.

strength, but his superior in wisdom; Matoschkin surpassed him in gravity. The latter used to sit for hours in a moody manner on a pile of chests looking at the ice world. Bop and Matoschkin were Newfoundlands; the first died of cold in our first winter, the latter, as our readers may remember, was carried off by a bear and torn to pieces. We had also two Newfoundland bitches, who were called respectively "Novaya" and "Zemlya;" the former died in the first year, the latter though she was of little use in sledging from her laziness, may claim indisputably the merit of being the mother of her hopeful son, "Torossy," who grew to a considerable size, and was the pride of the whole crew. He knew no other world than the frozen ocean, and no other destiny than to draw a sledge; and to this work he had devoted himself zealously since the commencement of winter. In the happy courage of ignorance he wagged his tail all day on deck; wagged his tail as he followed us on the ice; wagged it, even when Sumbu stole his dinner; wagged it even before the jaws of a bear. Gillis, the fifth Newfoundland, was incessantly quarrelling, and was the irreconcilable enemy of Jubinal; he was a favourite with no one, chiefly because he had killed the two cats which we brought from Tromsö as pets for the dogs. His body was covered with scars, and half his time was spent under the medical treatment of the Tyrolese. He was not wanting in docility but he was essentially an eye-pleaser; all his efforts in the sledge were mere sham. Pekel, the Lapp, was the smallest of all the dogs. In his early days he had tended the rein-deer at the North Cape and on the plains of Tana Elf, and his ways did not fit him for life amid the ice, but for the brown herd which roamed at the foot of Kilpis. Hence he was quarrelsome, and showed special enmity to Sumbu, the mere sight of whom was enough to stir up the most hostile feelings. He was therefore banished with his house to a high ice-cliff, but the thaw destroying its supports, house and dog fell plump into an ice lake. Among all the dogs there was no such desperate hypocrite as Sumbu, the most demonstrative in his friendship, but withal the most greedy and dissatisfied. He was the first to slink away with tail between his legs and find out the most secluded nook, when he saw the other dogs being harnessed in the sledges, and, when pulled out and put in a team, at once laid himself down on the sledge, not to draw but to be drawn. When at last he was set in motion, he was no longer the same dog. He was then full of action, unsurpassed in speed and agility, and his sportiveness was as great as his cunning. From the carpenter he would carry off a hoop, or a bag of nails from the stoker, or he lay flat on his belly and thrust out his long nose in the snow. His agility stood him in good stead, for it enabled him to catch all the mice that ventured on deck. Neither the stores of provisions for the dogs nor the depôt of food for the crew were safe from his depredations. He hated bears so fiercely, that he began to howl like a wolf when we turned out to hunt them. Boldly he followed up their trail even when at a distance from the hunters, and close to the heels of the bear. The dogs were fed once a day with bear's flesh or blubber, or dried horse-flesh, as long as it lasted.[1] They well knew the hour of feeding, and gathered together before it arrived. At night they were shut up in their house, and when the snow drifted they all lay huddled in a heap before the door. The dog-house was about eight feet high, but after a few weeks we could scarcely discern it from the accumulation of snowdrifts. For some time we kept up communication with it by means of a shaft dug in the snow; but one day in February a fissure in the ice was formed right across where the house stood, which compelled us to remove it.

9. The end of December came, and with it the season of those festivals which animate the Christian world— Christmastide and the New Year. In order to celebrate them in common, we built a snow house, decorated its interior with flags, and placed in it a Christmas tree, which, however, more resembled a wooden hedge-hog or a *cheval de frise*. About six o'clock in the evening all our preparations were made, and the ship's bell, sounding mournfully in the dark and misty atmosphere, summoned us to our snow house on the ice. Here lots were drawn, and cigars, watches, knives, pipes or rum fell to the fortunate drawers. For all these presents we had to thank friends in Vienna, or Pola, or

---

[1] We had brought 1400 lbs. of it from Bremerhaven.

Hamburg. Then came the Christmas dinner; but no one's heart was in the matter. Our bodies, indeed, were present, but our thoughts were far away with those we loved at home. New Year's Eve passed off somewhat more cheerfully. Better grounded seemed our expectation that 1874 would at last bring us our long desired activity and a not inglorious return to Europe. Scarcely had the new year begun than the crew knocked at our cabin doors with their congratulations, and such salutations continued to be the order of the day. On the whole this second winter, both before and after the new year (1874), passed away without the fearful events of the preceding. Although floes lay close to us on every side, and we had no harbour in which to pass the winter with comfort—like a bear in its winter sleep—the quiescent state of the ice allowed us to hope that our floe would remain in the position it had hitherto maintained. This hope, indeed, lay at the mercy of the winds; for if north winds should set in, it was extremely probable that the ice would break up and drift asunder.

10. The life we now led below in the ship had ceased to be in any way disagreeable, and cheerful and entertaining reading seemed to be healthier than bodily exercise. We did not suffer from any want of the necessaries of life; the temperature of our living-rooms generally admitted of

our sitting for hours even without our overcoats. The long night of this polar winter was gloomy and oppressive only to those who had time and leisure to weigh the burden of the hours. There were, of course, even in this second winter, some of those discomforts and dangers of

IN THE MESS-ROOM.

which the reader has heard enough, and which lead him when he reads of life in the frozen regions to think of ice-floes rather than of a room in which comfort is quite possible. We had, indeed, the usual inconveniences. As early as the middle of October the sky-light was so covered with frost that we could scarcely read even at noon. On the 20th of that month we were obliged to keep the lamps constantly burning, and to close in the skylight, which brought night into the mess-room before the night of Nature had arrived. By the middle of November the condensation of moisture was perceptible, and our bed-clothes were frequently frozen to the wall, and had to be torn from it before we could go to rest. Yet what signified all this? We all slept soundly notwithstanding, and during the day had to complain rather of warmth than of cold. The condition of the crew, however, was not so happy. We could not follow the example set by Hayes and others of removing the contents of the hold to the land, and so transforming it into quarters for the men. On board the *Tegetthoff* we suffered some of the evils of over-population, and the moisture was so much increased from it, that some of the berths were completely saturated. The employment of hammocks would perhaps avert this evil.

11. The number of those afflicted with scurvy decreased with the approach of spring. Their gums recovered their fresh and natural appearance, and the general weakness, the pains in the joints, the leaden weight of the feet, the depression of spirits—symptoms of this terrible malady—abated, and the scorbutic marks disappeared from their bodies. Pachtusow, when he

wintered in Novaya Zemlya, so abundant in supplies of drift-wood, caused his people to use the bath once a week in a log house constructed on the land, as a preservative against scurvy, and had their inner clothing washed twice a week, but even these steps were insufficient to avert the malady. In our case baths so added to the moisture that we were obliged to put a stop to them, and our under-garments could be changed only as our stock of them permitted. Hence we could hope to prevent the spread of scurvy only by the improvement of our diet. Several hundredweight of potatoes and a large supply of preserved meat had been kept in store for the second winter. These now came into use, and were the more welcome as our supply of lemon juice—the most important preservative against scurvy— was diminishing. By the advice of our physician, Dr. Kepes, we departed from the maxim, so generally adhered to in Arctic expeditions, of avoiding spirituous liquors. From the beginning of October our men daily received rations of brandy. When I compare the sanitary condition of the crew of the *Tegetthoff* with the better state of that of the *Germania*, I attribute this to the lesser power of resistance to disease in some of our people on board the *Tegetthoff*, and to the moral depression so easily explained by our disasters in this ship.

12. The Arctic voyager is exposed to no disease so much

as to scurvy. Its appearance among a crew exercises a most untoward influence. Its causes are still but little known; the means, however, of combating it are numerous. It is no longer the scourge it was in the days of Barentz, when he and all his men were attacked with it on the short summer excursion of 1595, or when in Munk's expedition of 1619, all died but two. In Behring's expedition of 1741, out of seventy-six men, forty-two were attacked and thirty died. In Tschirikoff's summer expedition during that same year (1741), out of seventy men, twenty died. Rossmyslow, who passed the winter of 1768-69 in "Matoschkin-Schar," lost seven out of thirteen men. When the disease gains the mastery, the utter incapacity of the expedition for further exploration follows as a necessary consequence. Lassinius, who was sent out to explore Novaya Zemlya in 1819, had to return in the height of summer, all his men having fallen down with the scurvy. This disease has been a frightful enemy to expeditions which have wintered in that region, and carried off numerous victims. All these, it is true, were miserably equipped and depended on the medicinal virtues of the "Löffel-kraut" of that country for remedies against the disease. In 1832-33 Pachtusow, wintering in the south of the island, out of ten men lost three; in 1834-35, two more died of the same disease. In the expedition of Ziwolka and Mojscjew, 1838-39, the scurvy gained such mastery, that at the end of February half of the crew were attacked, and Ziwolka himself with eight men died. Parry regarded damp, especially damp bedding, as the principal cause of the malady. During his wintering at Melville Island he found sorrel an effective remedy or palliative. He attributed the greatest anti-scorbutic effect to beer; and according to him and to most of the English expeditions beer and wine take the place of brandy. The disease generally has a fatal issue when there has been excessive loss of blood, or when dropsy supervenes. Most of Ross's second expedition suffered more or less from it, and the experience of that expedition showed that vegetable nourishment alone was not competent to make head against it. Ross regarded the addition of fish or seals to the ordinary diet as an effective preservative, and did not disdain the use of blubber for the same purpose. Lemon-juice, uncooked potatoes, fruit with much acidity, fresh vegetables and fresh meat, wine and yeast, exercise in the open air, and cheerfulness have always proved sufficient to prevent its appearance, or at any rate to render it improbable. But however valuable these may be as preventives, they almost cease to have any effect when the disease has once broken out. The lime-juice must be fresh, and, like vinegar, be taken in as concentrated a form as possible. It is decomposed and useless by being kept too long, and also by the action of frost. This was the case with the lemon-juice which Sir John Ross found among the stores of the *Fury*. An anti-scorbutic effect has been attributed also—and with justice—to the chewing of tobacco. It appears that liability to scurvy is very different among different races, and that neither vegetable nor animal food is an absolute preservative. The Eskimos and even the Lapps, who seldom or never use vegetables, are almost exempt from it, and McClure's men fell down with it in their second winter, although they had fresh meat three times a week. Steller relates that in Kamschatka scurvy attacks strangers only, but not the natives, who live largely on vegetables; he states also, that the scurvy, when it does appear among strangers and visitors there, is cured by a diet of the fresh fish of spring.

CHAPTER XIV.

SUNRISE OF 1874.

1. An unbroken sleep for the whole winter would, undoubtedly, be a blessing to the Arctic navigator, and the most energetic among us resigned himself to slumber for a few hours in the afternoon—the profane time of the day for all zones of the earth—especially after the coming in of the New Year, when the long unbroken night is intensely felt. The darkness diminished very gradually, and as the weather was frequently cloudy and dull, it was little lessened by the full moon, which we had at the beginning of January and February. December 26, we were able to read only the title of *New Free Press*, at the distance of a few inches, but not a word of Vogt's *Geology*. January 11, the word Geology on the title of that book was discernible in clear weather, but only when the book was held up to the light of the mid-day twilight. On the following day it was as dark at nine o'clock in the morning as at noon on December 1st. The moon returned again on

the 24th of January, and after it was four days old we could distinguish the common print of the "Press" by its light, and for the first time read off the degrees of the thermometer without artificial means. During the whole of the month we had alternations of high temperatures and snow-drifting, and at the end of it the wind dropped and the cold became exceedingly great, causing the ice to break up to the south of our position. The water-colour drawing[1] taken on board the *Tegetthoff* on the 8th of February may give some notion of the wonderful forms produced by the twilight, and its glowing colour-effects, but hardly any of the indescribable blaze of the meridian heavens, while deep shadows still lay over the ice-plains and a dark ridge fringed and closed the horizon.

2. At noon on the 23rd of February the rolling mists glowed with a red light, announcing the re-appearance of the sun. The next day the sun himself, raised and distorted into an oval shape, appeared above the horizon about 10 A.M. Again there was spread over the snow that magical rosy hue, those bright azure shadows, which impart a poetical character even to the landscape of the frozen north. The return of the sun was this year the deliverance from our long night of 125 days.[2]

---

[1] See the Frontispiece of this volume.
[2] Parry's winter night of 1819-20 lasted eighty-four days; Ross's,

Anxiously had we waited his return, and joyously we greeted it, but not with the frenzied feelings of the previous year. Then the reappearance of the sun was tantamount almost to a deliverance from hell itself; but now the sun was nothing to us but as a means to an end: would it enable us to begin our sledge-journeys to explore the Kaiser Franz-Josef land? The mere thought of the possibility of making new discoveries threw us into a feverish impatience, and our fears became intense lest the ship with its floe should drift away and frustrate the execution of our plans just as they seemed feasible.

3. On that same day Lieutenant Weyprecht and I resolved to abandon the ship after the termination of our projected sledge journeys of discovery, and to attempt to return to Europe by means of the boats and sledges. No arguments were needed to convince every one of the ship's company of the absolute necessity of this resolution. Our ship lay on its icy elevation, beyond the power of man to liberate her, and the provisions would not be sufficient to sustain us for another year. But fear lest the state of our health should greatly deteriorate in a third winter spoke more forcibly

in the Gulf of Boothia, fifty days; Kane's, in Rennssalaer harbour, 113 days, and Hayes' 123. In the latter case, however, the mountains on his southern horizon were the cause why the sun was not earlier visible.

than anything else in favour of our decision. When we looked at our medical stores, once so ample, now so reduced, at the few bottles of lemon-juice we could count on, all saw the impossibility of our remaining longer in these latitudes. The melancholy issue of Franklin's expedition forced itself on our mind as an instructive example and warning. In all likelihood that ill-fated expedition had delayed its return a year longer than it should have done, and began it in so weakened a condition, that it was next to an impossibility that they should have succeeded in their purpose. We began to be pinched also in many of our stores, in spite of the greatest economy in their use. To add to our perils the doctor drew a sad picture of the sanitary condition of our crew. Of nineteen men, several had fallen sick : Krisch still suffered from scurvy and consumption ; Marola from the first scorbutic symptoms ; Fallesich from its consequences ; Vecerina from the utter inability to move his lower extremities, produced by the same malady ; Palmich from a constant tendency to it and the contraction of his lower extremities ; Pospischill from lung disease ; and Haller from a rheumatic affection of his extremities which almost incapacitated him for any exertion.

CHAPTER XV.

THE AURORA.

1. THE Northern lights had shone for these two winters with incomparable splendour, not, indeed, with the quiet, diverging beams, sometimes observed in our northern latitudes, and different also from the phenomena which have been seen and noted in recent years, even in Central Europe; they resembled rather those we saw in East Greenland, save that the brilliancy and intensity of their colours were far greater.

2. It is very difficult to characterise the forms of this phenomenon, not only because they are manifold, but because they are constantly changing. Sometimes the Aurora appears like flaming arches with glowing balls of light; sometimes in irregular meridians painted on the heavens, sometimes in brilliant bands and patches of light on the sky. Each of these forms was frequently developed from a different one, but towards morning the last named appearance was the most general.

3. The movement of the waves of light gave the

impression, that they were the sport of winds, and their sudden and rapid rise resembled the uprising of whirling vapours, such as the Geysers might send forth, which generally assumed the form of enormous flames, except that they were transparent and mist-like. In many cases the Aurora much resembled a flash of summer lightning conceived as permanent. It appeared almost always in the south, and was visible from September till March, during which period it was to us the only external excitement which we had. The illuminating power of the Aurora, when its colours were most brilliant and intense, was inferior to the illuminating power of the full moon. Some rare cases excepted, this was either so small or so transitory, that it had no influence on the darkness of our long winter nights. Like a stream, or in brilliant convolutions, the light rushed over the firmament, as well from east to west as from west to east. The formation of the corona (or the convergence of the streamers in the direction of the inclination needle) was sudden and short in its duration, and frequently happened more than once in the course of a night. Its greatest intensity was from eight till ten o'clock at night. It was never accompanied with sound.[1] The sketch we have given represents one of its

[1] It has often been asserted that sound accompanying the Aurora has been heard on the Shetland Isles, and in Siberia: but all

Y 2

most characteristic forms. The inner parts of the flames are usually whitish green, and their edge on the upper side red, on the lower green.

4. Brilliant auroras were generally succeeded by bad weather. Those on the other hand which did not rise to any great height in the sky or which did not show any special mobility were regarded as the precursors of calms. None of the theories which have been ventilated are in exact accordance with all the manifestations of these northern lights. The undulating motion of their waves of light, their rolling forth like pillars of smoke driven by winds has hitherto remained unexplained. Although electrical processes, still unknown, seem to be the main causes of the Aurora, atmospheric vapours may, however, have a considerable part in producing the phenomena; and nothing so much favours this supposition as the indefinite form in which it often appears. Its occurrence during the day, *i.e.* light clouds with its characteristic movement, has been rather imagined than actually observed. The transition of white clouds into auroral forms at night has never at least been satisfactorily proved. Falling stars pass through the northern lights without producing any perceptible effect, or

scientific travellers protest against this. Franklin, who at first believed in this alleged phenomenon, afterwards retracted his opinion, and was convinced that the noise proceeded from terrestrial causes.

undergoing any change. A dirty sulphur yellow was characteristic of all auroras when the sky was overcast with mists or when it was seen by moonlight. In clear weather they were colourless.

5. Their influence on the magnetic needle was very variable. While the quiescent and regular arches had little or no effect, the quicker and more fitful streamers, especially when accompanied with prismatic colours, produced great disturbance in it. Sir John Ross remarked, that the Aurora when tinged with deep red colour had a great effect on it, although he completely stultifies his observation by his supposition, that the phenomenon was produced by rays of the sun reflected on the vast fields of snow and ice surrounding the Pole. Parry in 1820 could discover no effect from it either on the magnetic needle or on the electrometer. During the winter of 1872-3, the character of the northern lights was much altered, though their colour remained constant. At first they consisted chiefly of bands of light, running from the south northwards. At a later period of that winter they assumed for the most part the appearance of coronæ, and then their direction was from the north southwards. During the voyage of the *Tegetthoff* the observations of the behaviour of these lights and of the magnetic constants were taken by Weyprecht, Brosch, and Orel by means of a magnetic theodolite, a dipping needle, and three variation

instruments. The extraordinary disturbances of the needle rendered the determination of exact mean values for the magnetic constants impossible. The diminution of their intensity was considerable during the continuance of Auroras. In 79° 51′ N. Lat. and 58° 56′ E. Long. the declination amounted to $19\frac{1}{2}°$ E. and the inclination to 82° 22′. The ice pressures which occurred in December, 1873, together with the tedious preliminaries in fixing the magnetic instruments, prevented these officers from carrying out their labours regularly till the next month. The following are the principal results of these observations: (1) The magnetic disturbances were of extraordinary magnitude and frequency. (2) They were closely connected with the Aurora; and they were greater as the motion of the rays was more rapid and fitful, and the prismatic colours more intense. Quiescent and regular arches without changing rays or streamers, exercise almost no influence on the needle. (3) In all the disturbances the declination needle moved towards the east, and the horizontal intensity decreased while the inclination increased.

6. In spite of the extreme difficulty of describing the appearances of those fitful and changing lights, I believe that the following description of Lieutenant Weyprecht will be found equally faithful and effective:—

"There in the south, low on the horizon, stands a faint

arch of light. It looks as it were the upper limit of a dark segment of a circle; but the stars which shine through it in undiminished brilliancy, convince us that the darkness of the segment is a delusion produced by contrast. Gradually the arch of light grows in intensity and rises to the zenith. It is perfectly regular; its two ends almost touch the horizon and advance to the east and west in proportion as the arch rises. No beams are to be discovered in it, but the whole consists of an almost uniform light of a delicious tender colour. It is transparent white with a shade of light green, not unlike the pale green of a young plant which germinates in the dark. The light of the moon appears yellow, contrasted with this tender colour so pleasing to the eye, and so indescribable in words, a colour which nature appears to have given only to the Polar regions by way of compensation. The arch is broad, thrice the breadth, perhaps, of the rainbow, and its distinctly marked edges, are strongly defined on the profound darkness of the Arctic heavens. The stars shine through it with undiminished brilliancy. The arch mounts higher and higher. An air of repose seems spread over the whole phenomenon; here and there only a wave of light rolls slowly from one side to the other. It begins to grow clear over the ice; some of its groups are discernible. The arch is still distant from the zenith; a second detaches itself from the dark segment, and this is gradually succeeded by others. All now rise toward the zenith; the first passes beyond it, then sinks slowly towards the northern horizon and as it sinks loses its intensity. Arches of light are now stretched over the whole heavens; seven are apparent at the same time on the sky, though of inferior intensity. The lower they sink towards the north, the paler they grow, till at last they utterly fade away. Often they all return over the zenith, and become extinct just as they came.

"It is seldom, however, that an aurora runs a course so calm and so regular. The typical dark segment which we see in treatises on the subject, in most cases does not exist. A thin bank of clouds lies on the horizon. The upper edge is illuminated, out of it is developed a band of light, which expands, increases in intensity of colour and rises to the zenith. The colour is the same as in the arch, but the intensity of the colour is stronger. The colours of the band change in a never-ceasing play, but place and form remain unaltered. The band is broad and its intense pale green stands out with wonderful beauty on the dark background. Now the band is twisted into many convolutions, but the innermost folds are still to be seen distinctly through the others. Waves of light continually undulate rapidly through its whole extent, sometimes from right to left, sometimes from left to right. Then again it rolls itself up in graceful folds. It seems almost as if breezes high in the air played and sported with the broad flaming streamers, the ends of which are lost far off on the horizon. The light grows in intensity, the waves of light follow each other more rapidly, prismatic colours appear on the upper and lower edge of the band, the brilliant white of the centre is inclosed between narrow stripes of red and green. Out of one band have now grown two. The upper continually approaches the zenith, rays begin to shoot forth from it towards a point near the zenith, to which the south pole of the magnetic needle, freely suspended, points. The band has nearly reached it, and now begins a brilliant play of rays lasting for a short time, the central point of which is the magnetic pole—a sign of the intimate connexion of the whole phenomenon with the magnetic forces of the earth. Round the magnetic pole short rays flash and flare on all sides; prismatic colours are discernible on all their edges; longer and shorter rays alternate with each other; waves of light roll round it as a centre. What we see is the auroral corona; and it is almost always seen when a band passes over the magnetic pole. This peculiar phenomenon lasts but a short time—the band now lies on the northern side of the firmament; gradually it sinks and pales as it sinks; it returns again to the south to change and play as before. So it goes on for hours; the aurora incessantly changes place, form and intensity. It often entirely disappears for a short time only to appear again suddenly, without the observers clearly perceiving how it came and where it went: simply— it is there.

"But the band is often seen in a perfectly different form. Frequently it consists of single rays, which, standing close together, point in an almost parallel direction towards the magnetic pole. These become more intensely bright with each successive wave of light; hence each ray appears to flash and dart continually, and their green and red edges dance up and down as the waves of light run through them. Often again the rays extend through the whole length of the band and reach almost up to the magnetic pole. These are sharply marked but lighter in colour than the band itself, and in this particular form they are at some distance from each other. Their colour is yellow, and it seems as if thousands of slender threads of gold were stretched across the firmament. A glorious veil of transparent light is spread over the starry heavens; the threads of light with which this veil is woven are distinctly marked on the dark background; its lower border is a broad intensely white band, edged with green and red, which twists and turns in constant motion. A violet-coloured auroral vapour is often seen simultaneously on different parts of the sky.

"Or again, there has been tempestuous weather, and it is now—let us suppose—passing away. Below on the ice the wind has fallen, but the clouds are still driving rapidly across the sky, so that in the upper regions its force is not yet laid. Over the ice it becomes somewhat clear; behind the clouds appears an aurora amid the darkness of the night. Stars twinkle here and there; through the openings of the clouds we see the dark firmament and the rays of the aurora chasing one another towards the zenith. The heavy clouds disperse; mist-like masses drive on before the wind. Fragments of the northern lights are strewn on every side; it seems, as if the storm had torn the aurora bands to tatters and was driving them hither and thither across the sky. These threads change form and place with incredible rapidity. Here is one! lo, it is gone! scarcely has it vanished before it appears again in another place. Through these fragments drive the waves of light; one moment they are scarcely visible, in the next they shine with intense brilliancy. But their light is no longer that glorious pale green, it is a dull yellow. It is often difficult to distinguish what is aurora and what is vapour the illuminated mists as they fly past are scarcely distinguishable from the auroral vapour which comes and goes on every side.

"But, again, another form. Bands of every possible form and intensity have been driving over the heavens. It is now eight o'clock at night, the hour of the greatest intensity of the northern lights. For a moment some bundles of rays only are to be seen in the sky. In the south a faint scarcely-observable band lies close to the horizon. All at once it rises rapidly and spreads east and west. The waves of light begin to dart and shoot; some rays mount towards the zenith. For a short time it remains stationary, then suddenly springs to life. The waves of light drive violently from east to west; the edges assume a deep red and green colour, and dance up and down. The rays shoot up more rapidly; they become shorter; all rise together and approach nearer and nearer to the magnetic pole. It looks as if there were a race among the rays, and that each aspired to reach the pole first. And now the point is reached, and they shoot out on every side, to the north and the south, to the east and the west. Do the rays shoot from above downwards, or from below upwards? Who can distinguish? From the centre issues a sea of flames; is that sea red, white, or green? Who can say—it is all three colours at the same moment! The rays reach almost to the horizon; the whole sky is in flames. Nature displays before us such an exhibition of fireworks as transcends the powers of imagination to conceive. Involuntarily we listen; such a spectacle must we think be accompanied with sound. But unbroken stillness prevails, not the least sound strikes on the ear. Once more it becomes clear over the ice, and the whole phenomenon has disappeared with the same inconceivable rapidity with which it came, and gloomy night has again stretched her dark veil over everything. This was the aurora of the coming storm—the aurora in its fullest splendour. No pencil can draw it, no colours can paint it, and no words can describe it in all its magnificence. And here below stand we poor men, and speak of knowledge and progress, and pride ourselves on the understanding with which we extort from Nature her mysteries. We stand and gaze on the mystery which Nature has written for us in flaming letters on the dark vault of night, and ultimately we can only wonder and confess that, in truth, we know nothing of it."

END OF VOL I.

LONDON:
R. CLAY, SONS, AND TAYLOR, PRINTERS,
BREAD STREET HILL,
QUEEN VICTORIA STREET.

www.ingramcontent.com/pod-product-compliance
Lightning Source LLC
Chambersburg PA
CBHW032044220426
43664CB00008B/855